Praise for *Requiem with Yellow Butterflies*

Australia and Latin America enter into a mutually illuminating dialogue in Halford's travel essays, with their engagingly unheroic protagonist.

J.M. COETZEE

Literary in the best sense of the word – attentive to place, inventive in its descriptions and bold in its disclosures.

GAIL JONES

At its heart, *Requiem with Yellow Butterflies* is a deeply loving portrait of South America, and of the often unexpected currents that flow from its shores to our own. James is a writer who wants to hear and to learn, and so inevitably his travels bring him closer to the lives of the continent's many brilliant writers and the extraordinary cultures that produced them. He collects their stories, and along the way seeks out the first steps of his own – as a writer, traveller, husband and father.

KÁRI GÍSLASON

REQUIEM

WITH

YELLOW

BUTTERFLIES

ABOUT THE AUTHOR

James Halford is a Brisbane writer who has spent extended periods in Latin America and often writes about the region. His fiction, creative nonfiction and criticism have been published in *Best Australian Stories*, *Meanjin* and *Sydney Review of Books*. He holds a literature degree and a creative doctorate from the University of Queensland, where he now teaches, and has studied Spanish in Argentina, Mexico and Spain.

REQUIEM

WITH

YELLOW

BUTTERFLIES

JAMES

HALFORD

UWA PUBLISHING

First published in 2019 by
UWA Publishing
Crawley, Western Australia 6009
www.uwap.uwa.edu.au

UWAP is an imprint of UWA Publishing,
a division of The University of Western Australia.

THE UNIVERSITY OF
WESTERN
AUSTRALIA

ISBN: 978-1-76080-013-0

A catalogue record for this
book is available from the
National Library of Australia

The epigram on p. vii is from F. Nietzsche in E. Bertram,
Nietzsche: Attempt at a Mythology,
R. E. Norton (trans.), University of Illinois Press, Chicago, 2009, p. 220.

Cover design by Alissa Dinallo
Cover image by Shutterstock
Typeset in 11 pt Bembo by Lasertype
Printed by McPherson's Printing Group

uwapublishing

MIX
Paper from
responsible sources
FSC® C001695

Contents

Requiem with Yellow Butterflies   1

Caracas   25

We Want Them Alive   37

Roraima & Manaus   61

Don't Care if It Ever Rains Again   71

And the Village Was Fair to Look upon   83

Redcliffe   101

Old Peak, Young Peak   107

Uluru: How to Travel Without Seeing   131

Porto Velho & Brasilia   147

Coetzee in Buenos Aires   155

Parque Lezama   165

Such Loneliness in That Gold   175

San Miguel del Monte   197

The Lakeside House   209

Notes   239

Acknowledgements   253

To rediscover the South in oneself…
– Nietzsche

Requiem with Yellow Butterflies

...a feeling as primitive and as simple as that of love.[1]
– Gabriel García Márquez

In faraway Brisbane, news reached me within an hour.

'Gabo died today,' said a familiar female voice down the line. 'I thought you'd want to know.'

It had been more than a year since we were in touch.

'R, is that you?'

'*Se murió en su casa en México.*'

'That's sad.'

She seemed to be calling from her Skype account; my office phone didn't recognise the number.

'Where are you?'

'They're leaving flowers and books and paper butterflies outside his house. He died of pneumonia.'

'You're outside his house?'

I whispered to avoid annoying my work colleagues. Aside from fingers punching keys, the office was silent. It was ten o'clock on Friday morning in Australia, Thursday evening in Mexico.

'Do you remember the yellow butterflies?' she said.

'I'm not sure.'

'I've tried and tried, but I can't remember that part. Anyway, people are hanging strings of them outside his house.'

I dimly recalled an image of butterflies fluttering over a couple making love in the bath. But my clearest memories of *One Hundred Years of Solitude* were of us. We'd read it together across a year of long, lazy Sunday morning sessions in bed, sunlight streaming through the window of our sixth-floor apartment by the muddy Brisbane River. I'd read the novel aloud for her, cover to cover, in the hard-won, mongrel Spanish I'd learned over years travelling and working in Latin America, while she corrected my pronunciation and patiently explained every unfamiliar word ('*el revoloteo de una mariposa*'). That was her fifth year in Australia, her third living with me, and we both knew there would be no further extensions to her PhD scholarship. A few months after we finished reading *Cien años de soledad* she submitted her thesis. The conditions of her Mexican scholarship required her to return home and work for a year. We discussed me quitting my day job to follow her:

'We could go back to Oaxaca in the new year,' she said. 'To that village in the sierra with the beautiful little chapel.'

'It's too soon. I've told you.'

The day of her flight, we lingered on the boardwalk in the Botanic Gardens until the tide exposed the mangroves below. They have a word in Mexico for an embrace so tight it hurts: *un abrazo rompecostillas*, a rib-cracker.

'I remember a lot of things,' I said. 'But I don't remember the butterflies.'

After García Márquez died, I found myself emailing and chatting with R nearly every day. We sent each other links to articles about him as a pretext, but we both knew what was really happening. Once we started looking, we found yellow butterflies in nearly all the memorials around the world, but never any explanation of their significance or where they'd appeared in the novel. Our Spanish Royal Academy fortieth-anniversary edition of *One Hundred Years of Solitude* was still on my bookshelf. But the thought of opening its dark-green cover pained me. We promised that somewhere in the world, at some unspecified point in time, we'd sit together with our old copy of the book and go butterfly hunting. For now, she wouldn't even tell me where she was living, or where she'd found work.

'*No importa*. You made your choice. You decided not to come.'

As I read the memorials from around the world, a spark of curiosity kindled. I was struck by how little impact academic critiques of authorship have made on popular portrayals of it. Since the 1960s, much professional criticism has emphasised readers' interpretive freedom and down-played authorial intention. Yet nearly all the coverage of Gabo's death, even in the quality press, returned to good old-fashioned biographical criticism, reinscribing the myth of the author-genius. Much of it described him as a 'universal writer' and his work as 'universal literature', without seriously considering what these categories mean or how they are constructed. The popular press focused on García Márquez as a global brand name and commodity whose prestige derived from the marketplace – more than 25 million copies of *One Hundred Years of Solitude* sold in over

30 languages – and from famous, powerful admirers like Bill Clinton, King Juan Carlos of Spain, and Fidel Castro.

When I started reading the obituaries for Gabo at the local, national, Latin American and international levels, I found something quite different. I encountered a series of culturally particular and contested versions of Gabo/García Márquez. In Colombia, his death occasioned soul-searching about negative perceptions of the country internationally; in Mexico, he was celebrated as an immigrant success story – someone who had made a better life in their country for a change; in Spain, at a moment of profound cultural pessimism sparked by the economy, the death of the 'new Cervantes' became an elegy for the illustrious Hispanic past. Meanwhile, in the English-speaking world, especially the USA, the obituaries played out a range of stereotypes, fantasies and fears about Latin America that have lingered since the end of the Cold War.

Working my way through all those different Gabos eventually led me back to R.

In Aracataca, where the writer was born, the memorial was staged largely for the benefit of the visiting media. On the Monday after his death, a symbolic funeral was held and screened on national television. A few distant relatives were present, but no one from García Márquez's immediate family. Some residents felt abandoned and grumbled that their most famous son should have done more to help the underdeveloped town economically. The municipal government embraced the celebration regardless, hanging yellow paper butterflies from the town's main buildings: the García Márquez Museum, the García Márquez school, and the Macondo residences (named after Gabo's fictionalised Aracataca). This community of roughly 25,000 people was once economically reliant on banana plantations. For the best part of 60 years, the United Fruit Company, which Gabo excoriated in *One Hundred Years of Solitude* for its exploitation of local workers and brutal repression of organised labour, was the cornerstone of the local economy. The company's withdrawal in the early 1970s prompted a financial downturn from which the town has never fully recovered.

In recent decades, Aracataca has enjoyed a modest resurgence due to African palm plantations, and a little Nobel Prize–related tourism. Attempts to convert the town into a living García Márquez museum, however, haven't been wholly successful. In a 2006 poll, a slim majority voted to rename the town Aracataca-Macondo, but the total votes were insufficient to make the change law. Around the same time, a Dutch expatriate succeeded in establishing a guesthouse for tourists. But when the owner publicly criticised the town's inconsistent water supply, the provincial government withdrew financial support. Shortly after shutting down the main accommodation option in town, the mayor erected an oversize English sign for tourists beside the main road: 'Welcome to Aracataca-Macondo, Nobel Land' – a gesture of grandiose futility that might have pleased José Arcadio Buendía, the impractical patriarch of the Buendía family.

Aracataca's memorial for Gabo was similarly shambolic. Heavy rain turned the decorative butterflies to mush, the main street to mud. Until a few minutes beforehand, it was unclear if the event would happen at all. Eventually, a procession of school students and a marching band picked their way through puddles and fallen mangoes, watched by a disappointingly small crowd. The literature teacher from the local high school read a eulogy. Due to technical problems only a short segment was able to be televised. Locals kept asking visiting journalists when the authorities would send Gabo's ashes. People wanted to know why the great man hadn't come home to be buried.

Days earlier, José Gabriel Ortíz, the Colombian ambassador to Mexico, where Gabo had lived for more than 50 years, sparked a minor diplomatic dispute by suggesting on television that the writer's ashes be divided between the two countries. Colombian President Juan Manuel Santos, in full campaign mode ahead of the May 2014 elections, took up the theme. His eulogy appealed to national pride. García Márquez was 'the most admired of Colombians,'[2] he said. 'They [Mexican authorities] know perfectly well we Colombians would like to have the ashes, but we will respect the wishes of his family. Those who say Gabo turned his back on Aracataca and Colombia are mistaken. Glory to him who brought us most glory.'[3]

In December 2015, after nearly two years of negotiations, Gabo's ashes *were* eventually transported to Cartagena, the coastal Colombian city where he still kept a house. But this looked unlikely in the immediate aftermath of his death. By six o'clock in the evening on the day of the memorial in Aracataca, the streets had emptied out. A few stragglers at The Leafstorm Café – named after García Márquez's first novel – watched the much larger Mexico City memorial on television, the only glimpse of the funeral urn they were likely to get.

Outside the Palacio de Bellas Artes in Mexico City, enormous clouds of yellow butterflies cascaded through the air. Despite heavy rain and strong winds, the crowd was large and animated, clutching photos of the writer, playing the trumpet, adapting the *grito* of Mexican Independence for the occasion:

'¡*Viva Gabo!*'

Eduardo Zalamea Borda, an editor at the Colombian newspaper *El Espectador*, invented the nickname while García Márquez was a journalist for the paper in the 1950s. In Mexico City, more than 60 years on, it was cheered by thousands of strangers. After queuing patiently in the rain for up to six hours, mourners were allowed inside in groups of 50 to sight the urn and lay tributes of yellow roses and butterflies. Those unable to enter watched the ceremony on giant screens set up outside.

With a high-domed ceiling, plush red carpets and wall-sized murals by Diego Rivera decorating its interior, the Palacio de Bellas Artes is an opulent setting. Many of Mexico's most notable cultural figures have been memorialised here, among them García Márquez's good friend Carlos Fuentes, who died in 2012. But the formal ceremony was at odds with the writer's common touch. 'Gabo would have liked less solemnity and more white clothing,' wrote local journalist Juan Cruz.[4]

The most energetic moment of the night was the appearance of a live band playing upbeat Colombian *Vallenatos*, selected by García Márquez's sons, Gonzalo and Rodrigo. The least lively moments were the presidential speeches. Colombian President Juan Manuel Santos wisely dropped the nationalism he'd adopted in Bogotá in favour of inclusive Pan-American rhetoric: 'Macondo is a new world and an old one at once where a peaceful utopia is possible – one we seek together.'[5] Mexican President Enrique Peña Nieto said it was a great loss not only for literature, but for humanity. He is not known as a reader. During the 2012 presidential election campaign, he was famously unable to name a book that had influenced him (other than the Bible). Between these two men sat Mercedes Barcha, García Márquez's widow. Dry-eyed and dressed in black, she fanned herself and chatted calmly through the ceremony. Her grieving would be done in private, but her presence bestowed a quiet dignity on the occasion that it would otherwise have lacked.

To understand how Mercedes Barcha came to be flanked by two presidents at her husband's funeral, to understand how García Márquez came to be celebrated as a 'universal' writer, I started reading up on his early days in Mexico, the period just before the 1967 publication of *One Hundred Years of Solitude*.

R still refused to tell me where she was living and working. But we remained in email and Skype contact.

'You should definitely write something on Gabo,' she said.

Legend has it that Gabo and Mercedes arrived at Mexico City's dusty central railway station in 1961 with only US$20 to their name. It was July the second: the day Ernest Hemingway took his own life. García Márquez's first Mexican publication was an obituary for Papa Hemingway, one of his idols. Literary modernism was dying and nobody was quite sure what would follow. Soon Mercedes, who had waited patiently through a 12-year engagement before their 1958 marriage, found herself financially supporting her husband and their two young sons while he wrote *One Hundred Years of Solitude*. The novel combined Latin American folklore with narrative strategies recognisably derived from modernist fiction in its North American incarnation (especially Hemingway and William Faulkner), but its global distribution and reception would make it a key text in the transition to postmodernism.

The 2014 obituaries in the major Mexican newspapers emphasised the young couple's upward trajectory in their adopted country: 'they were lost, undocumented, probably happy, but hungry.' Narratives of social mobility resonate well in Mexico, as anyone who's seen a *telenovela* will attest. Framing the couple's story in this way foregrounds a quintessentially Mexican preoccupation with the politics of migration in the region: 'Peña Nieto didn't say it in the farewell...but fifty-two years ago that woman [Mercedes] passed hours at the government office on Bucarelli Street waiting...for them to give her residency.'[6]

It should be recognised that the couple's poverty was, at least in part, elective – *la vie d'artiste*. It's true that politics was partly responsible for the move to Mexico City. Colombia was still emerging from *La Violencia*, a decade-long civil war, and García Márquez had made powerful enemies with his investigative journalism series, 'Story of a Shipwrecked Sailor', about a government cover-up. But the move was, as much as anything, a calculated risk by a highly educated and already accomplished writer pursuing the career benefits on offer in the metropolis.

By that time, he'd published a good deal of outstanding journalism, reporting from behind the Iron Curtain in

Europe, and from Cuba after the revolution. He had already published many of his best short stories, like 'Isabel's Monologue Watching It Rain in Macondo' and 'Baltazar's Prodigious Afternoon'. And he had published three 'Macondo' novels: *Leaf Storm* (1955), *Nobody Writes to the Colonel* (1961), and *In Evil Hour* (1962). The second of these – a bleak, deeply unmagical account of small-town dreams destroyed – is now considered a classic. But that status was conferred only after the global success of *One Hundred Years of Solitude*.

Irrespective of the literary quality of his work, García Márquez knew he needed to shift closer to the centres of literary capital if he was going to become a professional novelist, let alone a figure of 'universal literature'. Mexico City was not New York, Paris or London, but it was a regional cultural force (alongside Buenos Aires), and it was closely connected to North American and European centres through translators and polyglot intellectuals like Fuentes and Octavio Paz. The energetic promotion of Latin American writing in Europe and the USA was about to produce the 1960s Boom.

One enduring origin story about *One Hundred Years of Solitude* has Gabo and Mercedes driving from Mexico City to Acapulco for a beach holiday with their two sons in 1965. Gabo, an inveterate myth-maker about his own life, claims the novel's famous, time-collapsing first sentence – the one about the colonel facing the firing squad and remembering ice – appeared fully formed in his mind as he drove. At that point, so the story goes, having found the structure for the novel he'd had in his head for 18 years, he turned the car around, drove straight back to Mexico City, and didn't get up from his writing desk for 18 months. This little scene – the novelist cancelling the family holiday to work on his masterwork – gives such a good condensation of the single-minded and ruthless egoism we associate with a particular modernist archetype of the great male writer that it was surely invented or embellished by Gabo. Gerald Martin, the English biographer who spent more than 15 years obsessively researching every detail of García Márquez's life, says the holiday was cut short, rather than cancelled entirely. Still, many of the 2014 obituaries repeated it verbatim – never let realism inhibit magic.

In fact, the flood of inspiration lasted little more than a year. The novel was drafted between July 1965 and August 1966. Generations of fans and scholars have forensically combed through every detail of García Márquez's work routine across that period for insight into how the magic was wrought. The production of the manuscript, thanks to Gabo's mythomania and our own hunger for stories, has become a well-known narrative in itself. We know Mercedes worked to support the family and that García Márquez would drop their sons to school at eight in the morning, writing until it was time to pick them up again at two in the afternoon. We know that he two-finger-typed his drafts on an Olivetti typewriter, in a tiny office called 'the cave of the mafia' that was perpetually filled with blue tobacco smoke. We know that he corrected the manuscript by hand and gave it to his secretary, Esperanza Araiza, who typed it up, corrected his patchy spelling, and secretly read sections to groups of enthralled friends. Araiza was apparently so immersed in the story that a bus nearly ran her down in the street one day in Mexico City (again, this sounds suspiciously like García Márquez's fiction).

I suspect all the attention to the material circumstances of writing in Gabo's 2014 obituaries – what kind of ink did he use? What brand of cigarettes did he smoke? What colour flowers were in the vase on his desk while he wrote the great twentieth-century Latin American novel? – stem from a certain twenty-first-century nostalgia for the cultural authority of the novelist before the age of television and the Internet. The fixation upon these early twentieth-century artefacts conveys a longing for modernist authorship and its trappings: the idea of the writer as secular society's spiritual representative, and as a transcendent agent outside the market.

Looking back on *One Hundred Years of Solitude* from the vantage point of Gabo's death, we are also looking back on the dawn of the age of electronic media – not to mention the age of global celebrity. The novel tends to win comparison with works of high culture pre-dating electronic media: the Bible, Cervantes, Dickens, Melville. In fact, it was an exact contemporary of *Sergeant Pepper's Lonely Hearts Club Band* (the worldwide sales figures of the album and the book are roughly comparable). Forget Cervantes and Dickens, then, the best parallel in the Anglo-sphere for Gabo's blend of popular appeal and cultural kudos is John Lennon, whose untimely death in 1980 fuelled a similar outpouring of grief from fans and earnest hagiography from journalists.

It is possible to argue, with no disrespect to *One Hundred Years of Solitude*, that what truly marks it as a transitional work in literary history is its coincidence with the globalisation of the media and publishing industries. Certainly, it was among the earliest global blockbusters to have been produced by a writer of the so-called periphery. Gabo's opus arrived at a time when technological change was elevating the phenomenon of celebrity to a new level in the West and enshrining a new reflexivity in our culture.

García Márquez was an important figure in the shift towards what Joe Moran has called a 'meet the author' culture. Undoubtedly one of the most seductive storytellers of our age, he was also a masterly manipulator of his own image. In interviews and various published pieces of autobiographical writing (including his 2002 autobiography, *Living to Tell the Tale*), the story of his life is driven by powerful narrative archetypes: the starving, exiled writer and his wife risking everything for the sake of art, succeeding at last through love, talent and hard work. None of this is necessarily untrue. But to uncritically accept the author's own version of his life, as many of the obituaries do, or to focus exclusively on his individual genius denies the role of geopolitics. For just as Gabo's star was rising, the Cold War, especially the Cuban Revolution, was focusing Western publishers' and readers' attention on Latin America in an unprecedented way.

The marketing phenomenon of the Latin American Literary Boom was already well under way by the time Gabo sat down at his typewriter in the Cave of the Mafia. High-powered friends in writing and publishing, such as Carlos Fuentes, German Vargas, Mario Vargas Llosa, and Paco Porrúa, built anticipation in the Mexican, Colombian, Peruvian and Argentine media for Gabo's 'Work in Progress' (a name that deliberately echoed Joyce's long-awaited *Finnegan's Wake*). By 1967, he also had an influential Barcelona literary agent, Carmen Balcells of Seix Barral, who was a crucial figure for many of the Latin American writers of the Boom. The novel's initial print run sounds small in retrospect, but at that time, in that context, it was a risk for his Latin American publisher, Sudamericana, to print 5000 copies instead of their standard print run of 3000 (the run increased to 8000 two weeks before printing due to a high number of pre-orders). Within three weeks of its publication date, June 1967 in Buenos Aires (July in Mexico City), *One Hundred Years of Solitude* was that rarest of beasts: a number-one bestseller with a heavyweight literary reputation.

The process of going global took much longer than it would today, but momentum built steadily. Translations were published in Italian in 1968, French in 1969, and English in 1970. Unlike Jorge Luis Borges and Julio Cortázar, Latin American writers whose international fame was conferred by the French, García Márquez found his most receptive non-Spanish-speaking audience among English speakers. The *Times* in London devoted an entire broadsheet page to the first chapter of the novel. The *New York Times* praised it to the sky: 'You emerge from this marvellous novel as if from a dream, the mind on fire.'[7]

Such enthusiasm for his work in the USA might have surprised Gabo. Although he'd spent a brief period as a journalist in New York in the early 1960s, he was later denied a visa due to his energetic promotion of the Cuban Revolution through the Prensa Latina news agency. There were even death threats from US-based Cuban exiles around the same time. But increased US interest in Latin American writing in the 1960s makes sense in a geopolitical context, as translator Suzanne Jill Levine observes: 'The South American novel became important to readers in North

America because in 1959, with the Cuban Revolution, Latin America became a major player in hemispheric and world politics.'[8]

US soft power boosted the profile of many Latin American authors during the Cold War. It was at this time that Latin American Studies was widely promoted as a discipline in US universities. The American Association of University Presses, backed by money from the Rockefeller Foundation, set about publishing and translating Latin American writing. For all the talk of strengthening cultural ties and better understanding 'our neighbours to the south', there was also an ideological function to this activity.

Cuba's propaganda organs had seized upon the new Latin American narrative as a cultural symptom of the revolutionary mood they hoped would soon sweep through the region. Offering Latin American intellectuals opportunities in the USA was seen as a counterbalance, an important weapon in the war of ideas. In this context, the Centre for Inter-American Relations promoted Latin American writers through its literature program. 'Every Latin American writer who receives due recognition at our hands is a potential ally,' said translator Harriet de Onís.[9] Many gifted US translators, trained through these initiatives, went on to work for the large commercial publishing houses, such as Knopf, Harper and Row, Farrar, Straus and Giroux, and Grove, which would bring the Latin American Boom to English-speaking readers.

Unlike several high-profile peers, however, Gabo never renounced the Cuban Revolution, and never softened his criticism of US foreign policy – he more or less refused to speak English to the end of his days. It is ironic, then, that both of his outstanding English translators, Gregory Rabassa and Edith Grossman, should be North Americans who honed their skills under the patronage of the Rockefeller family. With Rabassa's help, *One Hundred Years of Solitude* lifted García Márquez's name out of the cultural moment that shaped him – decades of political violence in Colombia, the Cuban Revolution, US Cold War intervention in Latin America, the rise of a new urban middle class in Mexico – and made it possible to call him a universal writer.

Not long after *One Hundred Years of Solitude* was published, Gabo moved temporarily to Barcelona, with Mercedes and the boys in tow. His trajectory from the periphery of 'world literary space' (Pascale Casanova's term) to its traditional European centre was nearing completion. In 1982, he would stand on a podium in Stockholm dressed in a *guayabera*, a baggy white cotton shirt worn on formal occasions in the Caribbean, and accept the Nobel Prize for Literature. It was a gesture that asserted his proud Latin American identity. His acceptance speech, 'The Solitude of Latin America', begins by confronting Europe from outside, from the impoverished South: 'Why is the originality so readily granted to us in literature so mistrustfully denied us in our difficult attempts at social change?'[10] But by its conclusion the speech has shifted to talking of 'man' and 'humanity'. This is the moment of consecration, the moment Gabo steps out of the local, national, regional and Spanish-language contexts of his work and becomes García Márquez – universal author.

The rest is postmodernism. In the later part of his career, the novelist moved between Spain, Mexico and Colombia; he became a multimillionaire who could afford to keep homes in Paris, Barcelona, Cartagena and Mexico City, the last of these perpetually heated at 28 degrees to emulate the Caribbean; he continued to publish fiction and journalism, some of it critically lauded, nearly all of it bestselling; and he endured a level of media scrutiny not even his prodigious imagination could have foreseen. In the end, the 'death of the author' – if we understand this to mean the author's loss of control over the narratives told about his life and work – didn't come from radical reading practices within the academy, but from the postmodern media. García Márquez's name and image, by the end of his life, could be made to mean anything. A prisoner of his own success, he withdrew from all but a few press commitments, and would often answer questions: 'You'll have to ask my official biographer, Gerald Martin.'

Martin's *Gabriel García Márquez: A Life* is strong on detail but heavily swayed by Gabo's charismatic spell: 'If ever a subject was worth investing a quarter of one's own life in, it would undoubtedly be the extraordinary life and career of Gabriel García Márquez.' The biography praises even Gabo's last novel, *Memories of My Melancholy Whores* (2004), a book that may or may not have been written by an author already suffering from dementia. That work should never have been published. As Gabo's powers waned through the 2000s, it was left to his biographer to resurrect the Sovereign Author's God-like narrative control. In Martin's final chapter, 'Immortality: the New Cervantes', the cantankerous, elderly novelist employs the familiar '*tu*' as he cheekily summons King Juan Carlos of Spain to the launch of the Royal Academy's fortieth-anniversary edition of *One Hundred Years of Solitude*.

'You, King,' says Gabo. 'What you must do is come to Cartagena.'[11]

In fact, Gabo's death is a story of lost authorial agency. Just before three in the afternoon on 17 April 2014, Fernanda Familiar, a Mexican journalist and friend of the García Márquez family, pushed past the crowd in the cobbled street outside his home, weeping. Though she refused to answer questions, the press waiting outside the great wooden doors knew what was coming. More than a month had passed since his last public appearance (his 87th birthday), and during that period he'd been hospitalised for a urinary tract infection. He died like a king: holed up in his mansion with reporters besieging the gate.

Another family friend, the Colombian writer Guillermo Angulo, soon hurried inside, carrying a suitcase and wearing a hunting cap. He, too, refused to confirm the news, but at half past four it became obvious to all. A grey funeral car arrived, company logos covered in an effort to keep the location of the ceremony secret. The paper covering had become transparent with the humidity, and journalists were able to make out the text below: 'García López Funerals'. As the vehicle departed, someone picked a bougainvillea flower from the vine growing between the building's barred ground-floor windows and lobbed it onto the roof of the car. A statement on behalf of the family soon appeared on Twitter, written by Fernanda Familiar. Gabo would be cremated at a private ceremony that afternoon; a public memorial would be held on Monday at the Palacio de Bellas Artes.

But the public couldn't wait that long. There were soon so many well-wishers on the Calle Fuego that a security zone needed to be set up around the main entrance and garage to keep them away. Candles were lit and left along the footpath to be extinguished by the afternoon drizzle. Six months later, when R and I made our own pilgrimage to the house, there were still offerings laid on the doorstep. The security guard across the street asked us what all the fuss was about. He admitted he'd never heard of the writer: 'But I will have to read him now.'

That security guard's impression of Gabo, like those of all his future readers, will be shaped by the writer's fame. Already Gabo's own narratives are hard to separate from narratives authored by others about him, most issuing from centres of institutional power far removed from the muddy streets of Aracataca-Macondo, and even from his adopted home of Mexico City. With the sale of García Márquez's private papers for a cool US$2.2 million to the Harry Ransom Centre at the University of Texas, US-based Latin Americanists can now pore over Gabo's manuscripts and private correspondence with Fidel Castro at their own convenience. Sensitive to the writer's man-of-the-people image and politics, his family took the unusual step of requesting that large sections of the archive be digitised and made available online. Meanwhile, journalistic accounts of Gabo's life and work, often full of half-truths and hyperbole, circulate and recirculate online, reaching an audience beyond academic critics' and biographers' wildest dreams, beyond even Gabo's book sales. 'With famous books,' wrote Jorge Luis Borges, 'the first time is actually the second, for we begin them already knowing them.'[12] Roland Barthes put it another way: 'the text is henceforth made and read in such a way that at all its levels the author is absent.'[13]

'Gabo died today,' R had told me. But I still didn't know where she was. Together, but still apart, we'd spoken or messaged most days for two months, watching word of Gabo's death surge across the Web like the stream of blood in *One Hundred Years of Solitude* that flows through Macondo's streets – under doors, up gutters, around corners – until news of José Arcadio's death reaches his mother. In 2014, the stream radiating from Mexico City and Colombia burst its banks. Tides of real or affected sentiment poured in from across the world, from politicians of the right and left to popular entertainers and the world of high culture: Barack Obama, Bill Clinton, Dilma Rousseff, Raúl Castro, François Hollande, Shimon Peres, Mariano Rajoy, Shakira, Mario Vargas Llosa. By the time the mourning subsided, thousands of ordinary people had posted tributes online: 'Men like him never die,' wrote Gerardo in Cuba; 'See you soon, Gabo,' wrote Rubén in Peru.

The fiction writer's obituary is a strange genre. By surveying the public surface of a life, it excludes precisely those sharply rendered, subjective, intimate corners of experience that characterise good fiction. A chronological record of life events, publications and awards received cannot, by its nature, capture the sound of a great writer's voice on the page. Even the obituaries that strove to imitate García Márquez's style in some way – emphasising sensory detail and personal anecdote – gave a sense of a hollow or absence.

Indeed, what emerged most clearly from Gabo's obituaries as a whole was not his personality as a writer or as a man, but the way every portrait of him was really a portrait of its author and audience. Colombians worked through their pride at his success abroad, their dismay at being abandoned. *Granma*, the official organ of the Central Committee of the Communist Party of Cuba, praised him as a defender of the poor and an 'indestructible' friend of Fidel Castro.[14] Peruvian journalists rushed out to interview their own Nobel Laureate, Mario Vargas Llosa, whose friendship with Gabo famously ended in a still-unexplained 1976 fist fight. Vargas Llosa's words were then reproduced in Spanish-language newspapers around the globe: 'A great writer has died whose work brought great prestige to the Spanish language,'[15] he said, neatly shifting the focus from nationalist enmity – the Peruvian versus the Colombian Nobel Laureate – to the two writers' common linguistic heritage, shared with their readers.

The English-speaking world brought its own variety of perspectives to bear on Gabo's death. US-based Cuban exiles were most critical: 'Only a five-star scoundrel would put his literary fame in the service of a cause as vile and malignant as the Castro tyranny,'[16] wrote Humberto Fontova in *FrontPage Mag*. The *Economist* grumbled about García Márquez's 'weakness for the halo of power',[17] while the *New York Times* balanced criticism of his closeness to Castro with acknowledgement that he sometimes personally interceded on behalf of political prisoners.

Tributes by various writers display the same kind of heightened reflexivity as the editorials, each a variation on the theme of 'how García Márquez shaped me'. Australian novelist Peter Carey argued in the *Guardian* that generations of overseas readers with no knowledge of Colombia have been 'nourished by their misunderstandings'[18] of the novelist's work. As if to demonstrate, he misspelt Macondo throughout. Haitian-born, US-based writer Edwidge Danticat talked about the impact of Gabo's work on her as a young Caribbean migrant aspiring to write fiction. And here I am in Australia, another link in the signal chain.

Strange that an old journalist who punched out his greatest work on a typewriter should be mourned this way: scattered across the Web. If *One Hundred Years of Solitude* was a book about the coming of modernity to an isolated Latin American village – the arrival of magnets, refrigeration, the railways, radio and cinema – Gabo's life, at least the narrative of that life the obituaries tell, seemed to be about the transition from modernity to what comes after. Born the son of a telegraph operator, he had made a living writing for newspapers, and he had died on the Internet.

Late one night after half a bottle of cabernet, I sent R a different kind of email. I told her I still hadn't found where the yellow butterflies appeared in *One Hundred Years of Solitude*, but I'd spent two months following their trail across the Web. I told her that I missed her, that I'd made a terrible mistake, a year back, in letting her go. I would fly to Mexico City and meet her, so we could light a candle and leave it at Gabo's door.

'Don't go anywhere,' she replied. 'Give me your new address.'

The following Sunday I heard a knock on the door. I went to answer it in my boxer shorts, my face lathered with shaving foam. She was standing on my doorstep with a sky-blue umbrella and a milk crate. Her face was thinner and her hair was cut short, but there could be no mistaking her. The crate was full of kitchenware and utensils I recognised from our time together in the riverside apartment: a silver bowl and a hand-mixer like the one Mercedes sold so Gabo could afford to post his manuscript to Buenos Aires.

'You're here,' I said.

'I thought you might want these back.'

I left her looking at the bookshelves – English books arranged by author's surname, Spanish books by country – while I put the crate in the kitchen and went into the bathroom to wipe my face clean. I put on jeans and a blue *guayabera* she had bought me years ago during a holiday in the Yucatan Peninsula. When I came back, she was sitting on the sofa, flicking through a green hardcover I recognised instantly.

'*Ya las encontré*,' she said, folding the page over.

'What did you find?'

'Can't you guess?'

I sat down beside her and gently took the book from her hands.

'I thought you were in Mexico.'

'I came back,' she said.

She'd been in Australia for three months and was living only a few blocks from me. Her postdoctoral position was not with a Mexican university, as I'd supposed, but with the Australian government agency for scientific research, the CSIRO.

'Why didn't you tell me you were here?'

'Why didn't you come to Mexico?'

I invited her to stay for lunch. She was delighted to learn I still made quesadillas with fresh chillies from our habanero plant. Light rain that had been falling since dawn grew heavier as we ate. It was belting down by the time we finished, a proper Macondo downpour. Her flimsy blue umbrella didn't stand a chance.

I invited her to stay and put on some salsa and we danced around the living room at half speed, remembering each other, a little solemn despite the energetic music, smiling occasionally but not speaking, avoiding eye contact. After a few songs, we moved to the couch and opened the novel to the page she'd folded over.

'You read it,' she said.

'Sorry if I'm rusty.'

The section about yellow butterflies was only fourteen pages long, but it brought Gabo's voice back to me in a way none of the obituaries had. We often think of reading as a solitary activity, but it is always an intimate act of communion between writer and reader. When the writer has recently died, it can be a kind of haunting, the return of a familiar voice we thought had left our life for good. That rainy Sunday as I read of yellow butterflies, I remembered the sound of Gabo's voice. I remembered how it sounded from my own mouth, every Sunday morning for a year, in the grave, old Castilian language it had taken me years to learn and which I now spoke with a Mexican lilt. A person with whom we can share *One Hundred Years of Solitude*, I thought, is a person with whom we can share a life.

Caracas

He who serves a revolution ploughs the sea.[1]

— Simón Bolívar, 1830

I flew into Caracas, alone, a few days before Easter. The road into town wound through densely wooded hills. From the bus window, between tree trunks, I glimpsed shirtless men with machetes cutting palm fronds in a clearing. They were lashing long and short stalks together to make crosses for the holy week processions. Sombre grey skyscrapers huddled in the valley, encircled by hillside slums. Descending into the foothills, we flashed past crooked, tin-roofed adobe shacks in tropical colours. The only hostel in town was east of the Parque Central, just off the Sabana Grande mall. It had an electric fence, gates topped with broken glass, and a scabby, sad-eyed, scarlet macaw that someone had trained to say '*Chávez! Carajo!*' in a cage on the rooftop.

I didn't know what to make of President Chávez or his Latin American socialism for the twenty-first century. At 24, I'd lived under the conservative Australian government of John Howard my whole adult life. My heart hoped Venezuela would live up to the promises of leftist campus activists in Australia. But my head feared the Tory newspapers were right. I was in Caracas to learn more. With limited language skills and no local contacts, it wouldn't be easy.

The other Australians at the hostel weren't impressed with Bolivarian socialism.

'This's a fuckin' nanny state,' complained Mick, one of a group of half-a-dozen rowdy young blokes from Sydney who'd stopped over on their way to the cricket World Cup in the Caribbean. They were incensed because Chávez had banned alcohol sales over Easter to reduce the holiday road toll. Luckily for them, and unluckily for the rest of us, they'd stockpiled enough rum and beer before the shops closed to keep them guffawing on the terrace until dawn each day. They played pounding house music so loud not even the cockroaches in the dormitories could sleep. With businesses shut in downtown Caracas, and a fair chance of getting mugged in the street, I was stuck in the hostel with Mick and his mates for nearly a fortnight, waiting for the Brazilian embassy to reopen and issue me a visa.

In April 2007, I was already three months into a question mark–shaped loop around Latin America. I didn't know what the question was, but I hoped to figure it out on the 7000-kilometre bus and boat leg between Caracas and Buenos Aires. Two years out of a literature degree, I knew I wasn't like Mick and friends, but I didn't know who I was. I'd delivered pizzas, detailed cars, stacked library shelves, been a conveyancing clerk and taught English as a second language. Nothing felt permanent: jobs, relationships, the places I lived. I'd decided, under the influence of too many 1980s travel writers – Bruce Chatwin especially – that the best place to figure myself out was the road. I wanted to learn about the 'pink tide' of socialist governments sweeping across Latin America. I wanted to improve my Spanish so I could read Latin American writers in their own language. I wanted to overcome my awkwardness with women. Above all, I wanted a period free of work and study commitments to read and make sense of my life – no travel companions, no itinerary, no hotel bookings – just a vague notion of travelling south for a year, watching the landscape change.

In the mornings, a few of the other guests and I helped the Venezuelan staff clear the broken glass and empty bottles from the rooftop terrace, and listened to them mutter darkly about the '*borrachos australianos*'. During the long, hot afternoons the museums were closed, I struck up a friendship with Valentina, a trainee primary school teacher from Belgium, who was a year or two younger than me, spoke six languages and played the melodeum. For more than three years, she'd been avoiding the final semester of her education degree – the actual teaching practice – by backpacking around South America, slowly spending an undisclosed sum inherited from her grandparents. Her shaved head made her resemble the Buddhist nuns I'd seen in Cambodia, and she wore an assortment of grimy, shapeless ponchos acquired on the road.

'What are you reading?' she asked one day from the hammock next to mine.

'*Absalom, Absalom!*'

'Didn't you say you're trying to learn Spanish?'

'My Spanish still isn't good enough to read proper books. Besides, García Márquez says Faulkner's practically a Caribbean writer. What are you reading?'

'*Transcendental Meditation* by Maharishi Mahesh Yogi.'

'That doesn't sound very Latin American.'

'Shut up.'

Ours was one of those friendships of convenience that characterise lonely travellers. Though we disagreed on nearly everything, a male companion made her life more comfortable, and I relied on her language skills. On Palm Sunday, we watched a broad-shouldered, square-jawed blonde in a miniskirt cross themself as a procession of pilgrims in purple robes bore a crucifix towards the luminous-white Romanesque arches of Caracas cathedral. The next day, we took the cable car to the summit of El Ávila, a peak north of the city, and looked towards Cuba across a washed-out sea. In 2007, all of Venezuela was, in a sense, looking towards Cuba.

'Do you think Fidel Castro's still alive?' Valentina asked. 'Or are they just pretending, like people say?'

'I don't know. I was only there three weeks.'

'Were people happy?'

'I feel like I barely scraped the surface.'

In Havana, I'd illegally rented a room from a school-teacher who hated the revolution.

'You can't read that here,' she said when she caught me browsing an anthology of Fidel's speeches and essays over a plateful of papaya. 'Seriously, if I catch you with it again, I'll use it for toilet paper.'

But her best friend worked for Prensa Latina, the state news agency. She took me cycling through the tobacco plantations and cane fields at Viñales.

'See how happy the workers are? See how beautiful life can be when they have real dignity?'

'And did they look happy?' asked Valentina, now.

'Of course. That's why she took me there. What does that prove?'

'I haven't been, but I'd like to believe…I mean, I want so badly for there to be a better way to do things.'

'I wasn't convinced…'

A couple of days later we rode the metro over to the Museo de Arte Contemporáneo, where they had a complete set of Picasso's *Vollard Suite*, a series of 100 etchings made in the lead-up to the Second World War. It was disorienting to step out of steamy, polluted Caracas into air-conditioned luxury. The Picasso etchings from the early 1930s are sensual and decadent: a sculptor and his model drink wine together, then retire to bed. But the tone darkens as the decade draws on. In *The Embrace*, a minotaur disrupts the sculptor and model's lovemaking to rape the woman. One of the final and most famous of the etchings, *The Combat in the Arena*, abandons the sculptor's studio. The minotaur confronts two naked toreros in a bullfighting arena. This is a direct reference to massacres in bullrings during the Spanish Civil War, but the etching, through its composition, also suggests a view of history as a turning wheel with violence at its centre.

The theme of cyclic violence was also at the heart of *Memories of February Twenty-Seven, 1989*, an exhibition of wall-sized, black-and-white Caracas street scenes by the photojournalist Tom Grillo. In these images, Grillo bears witness to the Caracazo, a popular uprising in the streets of the Venezuelan capital in 1989 that culminated in an army massacre of civilians. That year, when hunger, hyperinflation and a hike in public transport costs sparked rebellions in poor neighbourhoods, the military was called in to 'restore order'. They slaughtered as many as 3000 civilians. The Caracazo motivated Hugo Chávez's first attempt to seize power, a failed coup in 1992. As elected President from 1999 until his death in 2013, Chávez liked to say the massacre was the moment Venezuelans rose up against the neoliberal economic and political consensus and began their brave experiment with Bolivarian socialism.

Returning to the hostel with our minds full of hellish images – trucks laden with coffins, corpses lying on these very Caracas street corners – we were stopped by five police officers on motorcycles, just off the mall. They wore black flak jackets, carried bolt-action rifles, and wanted to see our passports.

'I'm sorry. I don't have mine on me.'

'You need to carry your passport. Otherwise you can be fined.'

The head officer rubbed his thumb and fingertips together for emphasis. Together, we tried to make them understand my passport was with the Brazilian embassy. We even showed them the receipt. But they didn't understand or didn't care.

'Show us what you have in your bags.'

Both of us emptied our backpacks onto the pavement. When Valentina produced a photocopy of her passport, the police seemed satisfied. We'd been advised to carry photocopies of travel documents in Caracas, not originals. Apparently, dodgy cops would often confiscate passports and force tourists to pay a bribe to get them back. I finally managed to locate my photocopy, but my heart sank as I unfolded the sheet and held it up to show them. A couple of months ago, in Quito, I'd clipped out the photo to make an ID card for a salsa class and I'd never remembered to make a replacement. The police glared at me through the hole where my face should have been.

'*Ya tienes un problema, joven*,' said the oldest, an officer with a neatly trimmed moustache who wore black shades under the visor of his helmet. 'You'll have to accompany us to the station.'

A stocky, thick-necked young policeman with a shaved head and tattooed biceps patted me down. Standing behind me, he thumped the heels of his hands hard into my back and buttocks. As he finished the search, he squeezed my balls and released them in a swift, stealthy movement, hissing '*puto*' in my ear.

'Fuck, mate. Take it easy. We don't want any trouble.'

'Get on the bike. Your friend can go home.'

Valentina was crying.

'He doesn't have any money,' she said. 'Neither of us have any money.'

A shopkeeper intervened. We were not, after all, in some gloomy alleyway. We were standing outside a shoe store in broad daylight in one of the biggest shopping malls in Latin America.

'Do not under any circumstances go with these men,' said the shopkeeper. He turned on the lead officer, speaking loudly so that others in the street could hear. '*Señor*, we have all seen you stop dozens of foreigners here today. What crime have they committed?'

'Mind your own business.'

'That is exactly what I'm doing. You are frightening away our customers. My brother is a magistrate and I'm sure he'd be happy to look into this matter.'

By now, a group of business owners and curious bystanders had formed around us. In the face of all the attention, the cops decided we were not worth the effort and roared off on their motorcycles.

'My friend,' said the shopkeeper, switching to English. 'We have enough problems of our own here. Please, be more careful.'

Valentina and I didn't dare leave the hostel for two days after that. It was cool and tranquil on the rooftop, once the other Australians had left. If you inhale deeply in Caracas, a hint of jasmine can be detected beneath the exhaust fumes. In the evenings, we sat up late, observing the street life from above. One night, a lanky, grey-bearded bald man, barefoot, with a peculiar rolling gait and a torn red t-shirt stained with engine oil, lowered himself onto a scrap of cardboard on the footpath. He crossed his legs like he was going to meditate, but then began smoking through a Pepsi can, muttering to himself, rocking back and forth. A well-dressed woman in her forties approached. She wore a clean, white blouse and black pencil skirt, as if she had just come from the office. Her left leg was crippled and she walked with crutches. Sitting beside the bald man, she offered him a pipe, which he packed with powder, lit and passed back to her. From her handbag, she produced an electric-blue butterfly mask. Her face hidden, she sat smoking in the alley with the hobo for two hours. They spoke animatedly, like very old friends.

'Maybe they knew each other in a past life,' said Valentina.

'Maybe.'

I pulled out my bus ticket to the border town of Santa Elena de Uairén to check the departure time: eight o'clock the next morning.

'You're really going?'

'Yes, I'm headed south.' I would go to Brazil first, then Bolivia, and Argentina. 'No flying. I want to feel every pothole and speed bump. What will you do now? Back to Belgium?'

'I don't know. Maybe I'll go south, too.'

For the first three or four hours the highway east of Caracas ran parallel to the coast, past mangroves and lagoons, through scrubby, arid forest. Around midday, just outside of Barcelona – an oil town nothing like the Spanish city – the sea came into view again, shining behind the tanks and towers of a refinery. Then we turned south-east onto Highway 16 and followed the Guyanese border all day, the towns thinning out, the road narrowing, the vegetation growing thicker. In the evening, still a few hours from Santa Elena, we had our second encounter with Venezuelan authorities.

The bus stopped at a military checkpoint somewhere in the Canaima National Park, where a soldier ordered us to disembark and fetch our luggage from the cargo hold. It had been hours since we'd sighted another vehicle. At the roadside, dense thickets hummed with insects, and two large tables were set up under floodlights at a wooden shelter. Everyone had to empty their belongings out to be examined by the bored, surly teenage soldiers. It took well over an hour for all 50 of us to file past, and they became steadily more aggressive.

'*Dinero, dinero,*' they said, when my turn came.

'I'm sorry I don't speak Spanish.'

An acne-scarred, smirking boy with a machine gun held Valentina's tampons up for all to see.

'Where do you put these? What else do you hide up there?'

A Venezuelan mother, travelling without her husband, was forced to knife open the teddy bear of her sobbing three-year-old daughter, to prove no drugs were inside. A Brazilian businessman who objected to being searched was ushered inside a hut by three soldiers and emerged, half an hour later, looking pale.

'Those sons of bitches took my watch,' he said in the silent interior of the bus as we rolled away from the checkpoint.

A few months ago, R and I chanced upon a food truck operated by a Venezuelan couple, Jorge and María, near our home in Brisbane's inner south. It stood bright-lit in the summer dusk on the asphalt outside a mechanic's workshop. Since the baby was asleep in the pram, we decided to stay for arepas. Jorge sat at the table with us as we ate.

'*Mexicanos*,' he said. 'I can tell by the accent.'

'I'm Australian actually, but my wife is Mexican, so I sound like her. And you're a real Venezuelan? You're not like these Salvadorans who keep opening Tex-Mex places because Aussies don't know the difference?'

Jorge looked genuinely wounded. 'How can you ask? Of course I am Venezuelan.'

'I visited your country ten years ago.'

'Whereabouts?'

'Caracas mostly. I also saw a little of the south.'

'You were in Caracas? You're lucky to be alive.'

'What part of the country are you from?'

'Caracas.'

34

He told me they'd been in Australia five years. His daughter circled on her bicycle, her pigtails flying behind her. She would have been nine or ten.

'Elena can barely remember Venezuela.'

I didn't have the heart to tell Jorge that this rundown industrial street corner, with two brothels nearby and a perpetual traffic jam at the lights, seemed like the closest thing to Caracas you could find in Brisbane. I tried to think of something to make him feel better.

'The south was beautiful.'

'You saw the Gran Sabana?'

'Yes.'

'They say it's the most beautiful place in the world.'

'You've never been?'

'I always thought I'd go when I retired. I guess I'll never see it now.'

I was too ignorant of history and too self-absorbed, in 2007, to predict that the exiled Jorges and Elenas would soon number in the millions. A few weeks in the country wasn't long enough to recognise the symptoms of a broader slide into chaos. Since then, hyperinflation and a crash in oil prices has left the Bolivarian Republic unable to feed itself. President Chávez and his successor, Nicolás Maduro, have consolidated state power by removing presidential term limits and cracking down aggressively on opposition media. There's been blood on the streets of Caracas again these last few years, from clashes between pro- and anti-government protesters. Nowadays the country looks more like a failed state than a regional powerhouse. I didn't foresee any of this.

I certainly couldn't have guessed hungry people would one day break into the Caracas Zoo and butcher animals for food. All the same, my hopeful view of Bolivarian socialism had evaporated by the time Valentina and I crossed the border.

I had two eyes and two ears, and I could sense the wheel turning.

We Want Them Alive

Ayotzinapa is shattered. Mexico is shattered.[1]

— Elena Poniatowska

Mexico City was a dream half remembered. Since our last trip, the legend had eroded the real memories, replacing them with volcanoes and earthquakes and pyramids and cathedrals and 20 million souls 2000 metres over sea level. But now I saw familiar landmarks and street corners: the post office at Echegaray where I once mailed a box of books home, the mini-van with smashed windows taped together that I took to Chapultepec every day for a month. Bouncing over potholes on the way to my in-laws' house in the northern suburbs, I rolled down my window to get the full effect of the foul air and snarling traffic. The tricolour flag fluttering over the ash-grey overpass, the fire twirler hustling motorists at a red light, the scent of charred pork wafting from a taco stand — every impression brought back the real city I'd seen, four years ago.

My mother-in-law turned in her seat.

'*Hija*, how was the flight? Will they extend your work contract in Australia? How long until James finishes his doctorate?'

R's father glanced back at us in the rear-view mirror.

'They look exhausted,' he said, sounding the horn at a car changing lanes. 'Stop bothering them. Let them eat something and have a rest.'

'Are you hungry?' asked R's mother. 'Did you eat on the flight? Do you want *chiles rellenos* for dinner? Should we go out?'

'Whatever's least trouble, *suegra*.'

R and I had only been engaged two months, but I'd been calling her parents my *suegros* since we started living together in Australia – somewhat scandalously – about five years earlier.

It wasn't long before my mother-in-law asked to see the engagement ring, a cheap brass thing from the Oxfam store made of the recycled casing of an American bomb dropped in Cambodia. We'd chosen it because, like us, it was an exploded thing remade. On seeing it, she clasped her daughter's hand with the kind of fierce love that's difficult to distinguish from fear. Her brown eyes glistened.

'So it's true?'

Her hair was grey now, cropped shorter than last time. She'd stopped dyeing it when she retired from medical practice. Since then, she'd been taking courses at private colleges around town, studying frantically for a few months, jumping to the next thing: psychoanalysis, homeopathy, landscape painting. It wasn't hard to see how her oldest daughter settling permanently in Australia might represent a loss to her. Her husband had been slow to leave full-time work; no grandchildren had yet arrived; her other two adult children lived in the USA.

'Yes, it's true,' I told her. 'But we haven't set a date yet. We wanted to talk to you first.'

It was nearly midday by the time we awoke. From the upstairs bedroom, we could smell wet eucalyptus leaves in the park behind the house. We might still have been in Australia. But downstairs, the smell of frijoles and corn tortillas on the stove brought us unmistakably into the here and now.

As we ate breakfast, the drizzle subsided, and humming-birds buzzed around the feeder in the garden – our parting gift last visit. Once we'd eaten, R and her mother let Lola the bulldog out; they raced into the garden, flipped her on her back in the damp grass, tickled her tummy. Her father and I watched through the window, washing and drying the dishes between us.

'I hear you've stopped teaching.'

'Yes, a couple of months back. The maths department at the Politécnico gave me a nice send-off. Thirty years is a long time.'

'What will you do now?'

'The city isn't a good place to retire: the pollution, the traffic, the insecurity. We've been talking about moving to a smaller town, but we can't agree where. You remember how she was nagging me about Acapulco? She likes the warm weather. But Guerrero is very dangerous right now. I'd prefer Pátzcuaro.'

'Isn't Michoacán dangerous, too?'

'Well, at any rate, we need to wait for my pension to be approved before we can decide.'

We sat down to drink *café de olla* at the kitchen table, the progressive newspaper, *La Jornada*, spread out before us. Since retiring, my father-in-law had read it from cover to cover most days. He discussed the news in long, immaculate Spanish sentences, as if leading a class discussion.

'You're visiting us at a very difficult time,' he said. 'It would be better if you didn't go out this afternoon.'

He warned that clashes between police and protesters might make it dangerous for us to revisit Mexico City's historic central plaza, the Zócalo, as we'd planned.

'Are the marches about Ayotzinapa? I'd like to go.'

'It really isn't safe. Protests here aren't like in Australia.'

R had told me that in 1968, as a young university lecturer, he'd defied his own father to participate in Mexico City's biggest ever demonstrations. Forty years on, though, his first instincts were protective.

The protests were about Ayotzinapa. On 26 September 2014, in the state of Guerrero in Mexico's south-west, municipal police picked up 43 young, male student protesters from the Ayotzinapa Normal School. They were never heard from again. The mayor of Iguala, where the mass disappearance took place, skipped town in the aftermath. He was accused of masterminding the attack, motivated by a long-standing grudge against activist students from the all-boys school. Mass graves were then discovered in the hills. But forensic testing revealed none of the remains corresponded with the missing students.

By late October, when we arrived, the federal investigation into the mass disappearance was being criticised just as harshly as the complicity of municipal authorities. Mexican

President Enrique Peña Nieto dragged his heels for nearly six weeks before agreeing to meet the disappeared students' parents at Los Pinos, his residence in Mexico City. The meeting took place at about the time our flight was landing. In footage leaked online, one father, Felipe de la Cruz, can be seen standing over the seated President and his colleagues, furiously berating them into a microphone. He describes how his 19-year-old son, Ángel, narrowly escaped the fate of The Forty-Three. The boy hid behind a truck as police shot his best friend dead and loaded the rest into patrol cars. Later, when Ángel took another wounded friend to hospital, they were refused treatment, and soldiers told them: 'This is what you get. This is what happens to you for doing what you're doing.'

'We've reached the limits of tolerance and patience,' de la Cruz shouts at Peña Nieto in the video, the President nodding along like a scolded schoolboy. 'We are demanding an immediate response, as Mexicans, from you, our President…Now that you've seen the anger of each and every parent, I hope that, like us, you can't sleep soundly at night.'[2]

There was no immediate response.

Following the meeting, the other parents voiced their anger to reporters:

'¡Hijo de su puta madre!' cursed Mario César González. 'They say our boys are dead. It's a sick joke.'[3]

'I'm pissed off with this fucking government,' said another father, who didn't give his name. 'And with all the people who are still asleep because nothing has happened to them. They're crouching down, hiding, letting it happen.'

But Mexico was beginning to wake up. As the November Day of the Dead festivities approached, solidarity marches demanding Peña Nieto take action were building in numbers around the country. '*Vivos se los llevaron. Vivos los queremos,*' the protesters chanted, carrying stark, banner-sized, black-and-white portraits of the 43 missing young men: 'They were taken alive. We want them alive.'

R and I did go out that afternoon, but not to the Zócalo. Instead, we borrowed her mother's little grey Chevy and drove to University City in the far south. Behind the wheel, she leaned forward, concentrating on the traffic and potholes, following an especially circuitous route to avoid avenues often blocked by protests.

'I know you think they're exaggerating, but they feel responsible for you because you're not from here. Worrying is how they show they care.'

'I don't think your mother's forgiven me.'

'Give her some time. She'll come around.'

R's alma mater, the National Autonomous University of Mexico (or UNAM) is the oldest and most prestigious public university in the country. Each year for the Day of the Dead, the various faculties celebrate the life of a great Mexican. In 2014, the students decorated the rim of an extinct volcano on campus with enormous, brightly coloured reproductions of Frida Kahlo's paintings, made of rice and beans. References to the disappeared students were woven throughout: 'We're missing 43.' Framed in this way, Kahlo's stillborn children, twisted bodies and gaping wounds gestured outward, beyond the campus. Everywhere we went in Mexico, we couldn't shake the sense of something terrible happening offstage.

The 43 young men whose disappearance in 2014 sparked Mexico's biggest protests for 40 years were from a very different background to my father-in-law and the urban university students who protested alongside him in 1968. This time the protesters were trainee teachers (*normalistas*) at a rural school in Guerrero, one of Mexico's poorest states. *Normales Rurales* (normal schools) like Ayotzinapa have a long tradition of social protest that extends back through the guerilla struggles of the 1960s and 1970s to the 1910 revolution. Their demands echo those of Emiliano Zapata in the twentieth century's first revolution: agricultural assistance, land redistribution, universal education and suffrage, and eight-hour workdays.

The poor have long had to fight for these things in Mexico, but protest has become more dangerous recently, with civilians often caught in the crossfire between the drug cartels, their rivals and the Mexican state. Since 2006, more than 200,000 people have died in the so-called drug war.[4] In addition to the horrifying number of extrajudicial killings of civilians by Mexican security forces, human rights groups have criticised the widespread use of enforced disappearances and torture.[5] More than 30,000 Mexicans are missing as a result of the conflict,[6] which has cost the US government more than $2.5 billion in military aid.[7] It is astonishing this kind of money continues to be thrown at the Mexican military given their abject failure to shut down the cartels and their history of excesses targeting civilians.

In 1968, during the infamous massacre at Tlatelolco in Mexico City, army and government-supported paramilitaries opened fire on unarmed protesters, killing as many as 300 people. In the 1971 Halconazo, outside the Santo Tomás campus of the National Polytechnic in the capital, about 120 unarmed protesters were gunned down. Annual memorials for Tlatelolco and the Halconazo often spark fresh violence between protesters and authorities. The night the Ayotzinapa students disappeared they were collecting donations and organising transport for a trip to the capital in October to attend a memorial for the victims of the 1968 massacre.

Given this history, when federal investigators cleared the military and federal police of all responsibility in the 2014 Ayotzinapa case, few Mexicans believed them. Authorities blamed the disappearance and presumed execution of the 43 students on members of a local drug cartel and a few rogue elements in the municipal police. But everyone knew the corruption ran higher than that. The slogan 'It was the State' was soon daubed on walls across the country.

After leaving the university, we met a couple of R's old work colleagues at a cantina, a cavernous place full of dusty bull-fighters' outfits in cabinets, where the waiter brought a tray of quesadillas every time you bought a beer. María and Lupe were tough, worldly, no-nonsense Mexican women in their fifties, both divorced and remarried with mixed families. They were not going to be easily charmed by a green-eyed foreigner. When R disappeared to the bathroom, they pounced.

'Marriage, huh? I hope you're serious this time,' said María, slicing a threatening finger across her throat. 'If you break her heart again, we'll take you out cartel style.'

'I guess you heard some bad stories about me.'

'We heard you freaked out when she wanted to get married. We heard you called the whole thing off after four years living together.'

Lupe scowled and pounded the knuckles of her right hand into her opposite palm. She took a long swig from her foaming pint glass, smacked her lips.

'We took her drinking at this very cantina, when she came home. We were ready to kill you. It isn't too late.'

'We have a second chance now. Things are better – even our therapist says so.'

'Your therapist?' said María. 'What about her parents? Have you explained what happened? Have you explained why they should trust you?'

'How?'

Lupe slammed the tabletop, slopping our beers.

'You can't pretend it didn't happen. You have to reassure them you're going to take care of their daughter...I assume you asked her father's permission before you proposed?'

I stared at them in guilty silence.

María shook her head. 'They must think you're an *hijo de puta*.'

'I think her mother does. But what can I do?'

'It's very important in Mexico to ask your *suegros* for their daughter's hand,' said Lupe.

'Isn't it too late?'

'*Hombre*, this is the perfect time,' María broke in. 'You must buy them a very expensive bottle of tequila.'

'Yes,' said Lupe. 'You must say to them: "*Estimadísimo señor, estimadísima señora*, I have learned it is the custom in this country to ask the *suegros* for their daughter's hand. Forgive my impertinence. Please accept this humble gift."'

When R returned, Lupe and María explained they were coaching me on how to smooth things over with my parents-in-law, and how to court a Mexican woman properly. They started requesting romantic songs from a trio of old-timers with guitars who'd come into the bar, and they improvised an elaborate speech to my in-laws over the music, riffing off the song lyrics:

'Your daughter is a precious stone, señor, a jewel of incalculable value. Give me her hand, I beg you…'

Once the scolding was done, we laughed, drank and sang together for hours. By the time we tottered home, they were teasing us about our wedding night and listing names for our firstborn.

R's parents were relieved when we returned home that night. A car had been set alight downtown. Demonstrators insisted that the masked perpetrators had been paid by police to justify dispersing the crowd with water cannons. Bigger protests were expected any day. It was a good time to leave. Next morning, we'd set out early to drop Lola the bulldog in the care of relatives. Then we'd make a road trip together, all four of us, to Pátzcuaro, my father-in-law's hometown, 350 kilometres north-west of the capital, where we'd pay our respects to the ancestors during the Day of the Dead.

That night, I sat up reading *The Night of Tlatelolco* by Elena Poniatowska. The author dedicates this work of oral history to her brother, Jan, who was killed in the 1968 massacre. Her account of the protests that year, through its selective collage of testimonial interviews, presents 'a movement of pure and incorruptible men' to whom 'no homage…is excessive'.[8] It is an idealised picture of the protesters, but a moving one. For the most part, participants tell the story in their own words: a political prisoner describes being interrogated and tortured; parents tell of their fears for their activist children.

Poniatowska's only overt authorial intervention comes at the very beginning, where she paints a dreamlike picture of the protesters as she sees them in memory:

> They are many. They come on foot, laughing. They come down Melchor Ocampo, Reforma, Juarez, Cinco de Mayo, young men and women linking arms in protest with the same joy they showed only a few days ago at the fair... they close in on the Plaza de las Tres Culturas [the site of the massacre]...they come towards me with hands holding banners, childlike hands because death makes hands childlike...all my life I will hear their steps advancing.[9]

At 82, Poniatowska was still protesting. Only a few days before we arrived in Mexico, this tiny, frail woman addressed a huge crowd in the Zócalo for nearly half an hour – fainting afterwards from the effort. Her speech consisted of a brief, precise description of all 43 disappeared students from Ayotzinapa:

> Felipe Arnulfo Rosa, from a peasant family in the municipality of Ayutla, is 20 years old. He has a scar on the back of his neck from falling over backwards as a child... They call 19-year-old Carlos Lorenzo Hernández Muñoz 'the little bean'...When they asked for blood donors in Tixtla he was first in line.

She concluded by echoing the Ayotzinapa parents' demand: 'They were taken alive, we want them alive.'[10]

Those words rung out across the country as the Day of the Dead approached. In Iguala, protesters torched the corrupt mayor's office and spray-painted the slogan on its charred remains. But we were travelling north, away from all that.

My father-in-law played Rachmaninov on the stereo as he drove his grey station wagon away from the strife-torn capital. He'd marched back in 1968, but he was older now, waiting on his first pension payment. In the back seat, with Lola the bulldog squirming in my lap, I wondered what it would take to make him march again. As we passed from the Federal District into Mexico State, urban sprawl gave way to fields of golden maize. Dense green knots of cactus grew at the roadside. A stall near the turn-off for the pyramids of Teotihuacan was selling ant eggs.

We dropped Lola with R's uncle then swung onto the newly built Circuito Mexiquense, heading west for the state of Michoacán. Although we were travelling further from Guerrero, where the mass disappearance took place, and from Mexico City, where the biggest protests would occur, Michoacán was far from conflict free. On the road to Pátzcuaro, we saw a small protest at a toll booth. Four scrawny young men in t-shirts and baseball caps stood in front of it, waving an indecipherable black banner. They were in their early twenties, but small for their age, without masks or weapons. They shouted slogans we couldn't hear properly over the traffic noise.

'This booth has been taken,' said one of them as we approached. 'Don't pay the toll.'

He was out of breath, his face pockmarked with acne.

'Thank you, young man,' said my father-in-law, handing over a coin.

The official in the booth had left the boom gate open. He waved us through without looking up from his newspaper. Just beyond the unarmed protesters' picket line, we saw eight black-clad soldiers with machine guns in the back of a pick-up truck. It was easy to imagine the situation turning ugly, as it had in Guerrero.

For many of us in more fortunate circumstances, it's hard to imagine a social context so desperate that parents and teachers encourage high-school-age students to hijack buses and block highways. Yet that is the context for the Ayotzinapa Normal School. It is located an hour's drive from Chilpancingo, the capital of Guerrero state, and two hours' drive from Iguala. For a week before the mass disappearance, the students (I have to fight the temptation to call them boys) had been stockpiling stolen vehicles and petrol at their school for their planned protest in Mexico City. They went into Iguala that night, by their own admission, to commandeer public buses.

Just before nine-thirty in the evening, municipal police began to pursue two buses the students had taken from Iguala's central station. When a police truck blocked the road, some of the students disembarked to try to push it out of the way. Blurry footage, shot by one of the survivors on his mobile phone, captures what happened next.

Three or four panicked voices shout in darkness: 'We're unarmed. Don't shoot! Don't shoot!'[11]

Then a muffled boom like a director's clapboard snapped shut, a wildly lurching camera, heavy breathing, the blurred red headlights of a bus.

'One man down,' cries the camera holder, his accent a countrified drawl.

Silence. The camera swings across grainy blackness, falls upon a prone form in the road behind a police car.

After the initial attack, the students still on the bus were loaded into patrol cars and taken away by police, the missing eventually totalling 43. Some of those in the street escaped. When they informed classmates at the school of the shooting, a second, crazy-brave convoy of buses was sent to Iguala, arriving at about 11 pm. Around midnight, the reinforcements, who were being interviewed by local press at the scene of the first shooting, were fired upon from long range by unidentified men in trucks. Three Ayotzinapa students and three bystanders died that night, in addition to the mass disappearance. Their bodies were left untouched in the street by a population too scared to intervene.

The image of the dead left in the Iguala streets reminded me of a passage from Malcolm Lowry's classic 1947 novel about the Mexican Day of the Dead, *Under the Volcano*. As R's father drove west, squinting into the fast-dying autumn daylight, I dug out my copy and re-read the scene.

Lowry's alcoholic British consul is travelling by bus from Querétaro to Tomalin to watch a bullfight with his idealistic young friend, Hugh, when an Indian is discovered dying at the roadside. He has been stabbed and robbed. Upon discovering the injured man, Hugh is all for hauling him aboard the bus and taking him to hospital. A 29-year-old orphan with an inherited fortune, Hugh has fled Cambridge in disgust at the British class system, and refashioned himself as a socialist, drifting around the world in search of a cause (it's 1938 and he's flirting with the idea of martyrdom for the Spanish republic). But the world-weary consul warns Hugh against getting involved, taking a swig from his flask: 'You'll only get hauled into jail and entangled with red tape.'[12] As the bus departs, leaving the Indian to die, Hugh studies the impassive faces of the Mexicans onboard, wondering why they haven't taken action. He finally attributes their passivity to the lived memory of violence:

> Ah, how sensible were these old women...who had made a silent communal decision to have nothing to do with the whole affair...Perhaps they remembered the days of revolution in the valley, the blackened buildings, the communication cut off, those crucified and gored in the bullring...There was no callousness in their faces, no cruelty. Death they knew, better than the law, and their memories were long.[13]

In Pátzcuaro, a special Day of the Dead market had been set up in the Plaza Vasco de Quiroga. The local Purépecha people still affectionately refer to the first bishop of Michoacán state as 'Tata Vasco' (father Vasco). His statue was decorated for the occasion with the giant, butterfly-shaped nets used by fishermen on nearby Lake Pátzcuaro. Orange *cempasúchil* petals were scattered in a circle around the fountain.

Among the market stalls, my mother-in-law explained how to differentiate between cheap, factory-made textiles and proper handicrafts. She was hunting for a present to give my parents.

'Do you think they'd like this?' she kept saying, holding up one or another exquisitely embroidered tablecloth or shawl.

'Yes, very much.'

But this wasn't a decision to be rushed. Mum and Dad had sent them a handwritten letter welcoming R to the family, and a USB stick full of photos of her celebrating various occasions with us in Australia. Now, we worked our way clockwise around the plaza, seeking the perfect reply. It became clear, once negotiations began in earnest, that a second circuit would be required. My father-in-law and I retired to the bar.

Over a cold Negra Modelo, he proudly described a little of the region's history. Don Vasco was brought to Michoacán in 1530 to clean up after the conquistador Nuño de Guzmán. First as a judge, later as bishop, Quiroga tried to resolve the Purépechas' complaints in accordance with his humanist conception of justice. With Pátzcuaro as his new capital, he established a series of indigenous villages modelled after Thomas More's *Utopia*. The Purépecha were granted self-governance and encouraged to develop handicrafts that would help them survive economically. Vasco de Quiroga's model of 'soft colonisation', put into practice on a small scale in Michoacán, never spread to the rest of Mexico, as he hoped. But an administrative system based on Utopian principles survived his death by 300 years in the villages he founded.

Sadly, as R's father pointed out, finishing his drink, Michoacán is nowadays better known as the birthplace of Mexico's drug war. At its outset in 2006, more than 7000 troops were deployed here to combat the cartels. The most powerful of these, La Familia Michoacana, responded by bowling five severed heads across the floor of a crowded nightclub.

'Death they knew, better than the law, and their memories were long,' Lowry had written of Mexicans. That deeply ingrained lack of faith in the rule of law has been evident in the public response to the Ayotzinapa case.

The official government theory was first put forward in November 2014 by then Attorney General, Jesús Murillo Karam, who was dismissed a few months later for his unsatisfactory handling of the investigation. His office has persisted with the same explanation. They claim that the corrupt mayor of Iguala, José Luis Abarca, from the Partido de la Revolución Democrática, the chief progressive rival of the ruling Partido Revolucionario Institucional, ordered local police to intercept the students to prevent them protesting at a function hosted by his wife. Iguala's former first lady, María de los Ángeles Pineda, has been revealed to have family ties to the main local drug cartel, Guerreros Unidos (United Warriors). Police are believed to have handed over the 43 students to members of United Warriors, who mistook them for members of a rival gang, the Rojos, and transported them in trucks to a garbage dump at Cocula that was regularly used to dispose of bodies.

'They killed them,' Murillo Karam told the Ayotzinapa parents at a meeting in an empty aircraft hangar at Tulancingo airport, shortly before he was dismissed. 'They threw them into a ravine, they followed them down, they lit a fire that lasted fifteen hours, they burned them. Later they collected the remains, they put them in black plastic bags, and they threw them off a bridge into the San Juan River.'[14]

Not one person I spoke to in Mexico believed him.

The women returned from the market bearing a set of delicate white-lace placemats for my parents, and a bouquet of marigolds for the Mexican ancestors. Soon it would be time to lay the flowers in the crypt of the cathedral. But first we made our way to the beautiful old courtyard house where my father-in-law grew up: all high, crumbling, white-washed walls and dark, bare, shuttered rooms. It had been empty for five years since R's grandfather died. For a long time, it was assumed the house would be handed down to the younger generation. But in 2014, the family reluctantly put it on the market. It was unwise, they decided, to hold on to the house out of sentiment, in such a dangerous region.

The central courtyard contained an overgrown grassy area where cattle once grazed, and a small orchard. Whenever R's grandfather visited Mexico City he would bring the family a bag of fresh lemons or figs. He used to bathe each morning with a bucket of cold water from the trough where the animals drank. Once, in winter, he broke the ice with a shovel and commanded his young son to wash himself with freezing water, until his mother cried: 'You're going to kill your boy!'

R's grandfather was a tough man by all accounts. Among the flower pots we found a rusty old knife with its serrated blade inscribed: 'Vanity, all is vanity.' Yet his granddaughters also remember him smiling as he allowed them to beat him, time after time, at checkers. Between the bathroom and the main bedroom was a handrail. After separating from his wife in middle age, he lived alone for the rest of his life in the huge empty house – a place full of stories that are not mine to tell.

At the back of the garden was a separate, half-finished, two-storey dwelling. The building was meant to be guest quarters for his three children, who had all moved to the capital to attend university. But a dispute with the builders meant it was never completed. We climbed a set of unrailed stairs to the second floor and looked over the red roofs of Pátzcuaro towards Bishop Quiroga's vanished lakeside Utopia. The clean air tasted marvellous after Mexico City. In the street outside, a security camera turned silently atop a tall pole. There were signs someone had been there before us. Empty beer bottles were scattered over the balcony, and I found a length of cut-off garden hose from a home-made bong. Over the fence, in the neighbours' yard, roosters clucked in cages. While the house sat empty, cockfights had been held in the backyard without permission. Now the property was on the market, the real estate agent had requested the birds be kept off the property.

'I hope it sells soon,' said my father-in-law, there on the balcony. But he lingered in the doorway when it was time to leave.

In the crypt of Pátzcuaro cathedral, cleaners were sweeping and mopping the floor in preparation for hundreds of visitors that night. My father-in-law led us along a narrow passageway of floor-to-ceiling vaults: the dead stacked densely, one on top of the other. With a key, he opened a safe in the wall. Inside was a square, wooden container, little larger than a shoebox, containing his father's ashes. He picked it up, held it in his hands, and bowed his head. Though they'd invited me, I felt I was intruding. Death and grieving are rarely so public in my culture. Stooping under the low roof, I rounded a corner to give them their privacy. Briefly alone, for the first time in weeks, I blundered into a vertiginous corridor, very brightly lit, where the dead seemed to go on forever. How would the parents of the disappeared feel that night, I wondered, as the rest of the country laid marigolds in cemeteries and crypts? How could they mourn without a body to anchor their grief in space and time? Today, the first of November, was the day of the innocents, and was dedicated to the memory of children who had died.

If the government's version of events was being heavily scrutinised back in 2014, it has since been completely discredited. A group of independent forensics experts from the Inter-American Commission on Human Rights, the GIEI, found the bodies of The Forty-Three could not possibly have been burned in the Cocula dumpsite as the Mexican government claims. Their 608-page report found insufficient evidence to prove there had been a fire of the magnitude necessary to burn a single body – let alone the inferno required to reduce such a large number of corpses to ashes.[15] The GIEI also found evidence that the confessions from gang members on which the government based its version of events may have been extracted by torture. The coordination of the attack and its targeting of civilians contrasted starkly with past gang violence in the region.

If you read between the lines of the experts' carefully worded report, a different scenario emerges. It seems likely that the students unwittingly brought on the attack by hijacking a bus carrying a shipment of narcotics bound for the USA (federal investigators excluded a fifth hijacked bus from their investigation despite numerous witness accounts). Evidence suggests that all captured buses were carefully monitored by federal police and the army across the night in question. Both agencies were present during the attacks by municipal police and at the very least did nothing to prevent them. It is most likely the bodies were burned in a crematorium so as not to leave a trace, the report states, stopping just short of a direct accusation.

But Jorge Antonio Montemayor Aldrete, a physicist at the UNAM, has had no such reservations. He argues the corpses could only have been burned at one of the military bases in the area – several of which are equipped with crematoriums. Aldrete has invited the Guerrero military bases near Iguala to disprove his theory by producing their gas bills.

None have complied.[16]

Shortly before midnight, in the cathedral over the crypt, the Michoacán Symphony Orchestra performed Brahms's *German Requiem*. Above the orchestra and the altar with its grisly black Christ, the Virgin of Health wore a red gown embossed with glittering jewels. Behind her glass case, the gown's long train extended to the back wall, above head height, so that the faithful could walk beneath it. The fabric was hung with hundreds of tiny aluminium figures, bent in the posture of prayer, each one a request for the Virgin's intercession. Tonight, a full orchestra and choir took the place of the usual petitioners. Since the concert was free, people from across the social spectrum were in attendance, from tourists and expatriates to local families.

As the choir sang, R traced the German text in the program with her finger, allowing me to follow the Spanish translation alongside. With her two siblings, she had attended the German international school in Mexico City. On the strength of that education, all three had gone on to university studies abroad, and had established professional careers in the USA or Australia. This was the Mexican dream. But what kind of dream is it that scatters a family across three countries? I had not realised, until this trip, how painful the separation was for all of them. There are many ways to lose your children.

A heavy mood hung over the rest of the audience, despite the requiem's promise of redemption. Many in the crowd would have had loved ones murdered or disappeared in recent years. They listened, stony-faced, to the choir. A few minutes before the end, a young couple entered. They were in their late teens, about the age of the missing students from Ayotzinapa, and both had their faces painted as skeletons. The young man wore a waistcoat, the woman an ankle-length yellow dress. Down the aisle of the cathedral they came, arms linked like death's wedding march. They weren't part of the show, only late arrivals, but all eyes turned towards them. Once they found seats, my eyes kept stealing back to the pair of beautiful young skeletons, who had entered to the blare of brass. The final verses seemed directed to them:

> For the trumpet shall sound,
> and the dead shall be raised incorruptible,
> and we shall be changed...[17]

My mother-in-law caught me drying my eyes. She smiled.

Three weeks later, back in Mexico City, it was nearly time for us to go home. While we were in Michoacán, the fugitive mayor of Iguala and his wife had been captured in a dramatic 3 am raid, and the capital had been rocked by massive protests. President Peña Nieto was at the G20 summit in my hometown of Brisbane. A local bar owner who posted Facebook photos of himself with the glamorous Mexican First Lady quickly removed them following abuse from Mexican expatriates: 'Shame on you. Her husband is a fucking murderer. He has blood on his hands.'

Meanwhile, in Mexico, protesters screamed for Peña Nieto's resignation, and masked men set fire to the 150-year-old wooden door of the National Palace.

Preoccupied with the chaos around us, we'd kept our talk of personal matters light. I hadn't yet brought up the engagement with R's parents. On our last night, I finally wrestled control of the kitchen from my mother-in-law, and was able to prepare a special meal.

'*Necesito hablarles de algo importante*,' I said as we sat down before four steaming bowls of Thai red curry. I didn't buy them fancy tequila or address her father as *Estimadísimo señor*. Even so, I felt María and Lupe would have approved. I told R's parents that I was sorry I had caused her pain in the past, that I wouldn't make the same mistake twice. I was committed to her and wanted, with their blessing, to spend my life by her side. The food was cold before any of us ate. My father-in-law replied with a short speech and presented me with a letter for my parents he'd written using Google Translate.

'Australia...Australia is so far away,' said my-mother-in-law. But she composed herself and gave us her blessing. They both did.

As I write, more than four years on from the mass disappearance in Iguala, only one of The Forty-Three has been confirmed dead by forensic evidence.

'I wish they'd left my son dead on the ground so I could fetch him,' said the young man's father, Ezequiel Mora. 'But all they've left me is a shard of bone and a molar.'[18] The parents of the remaining 42, lacking physical proof, continue the search.

'I don't feel that my son is dead,' María Concepción Tlatempa told journalists. 'When something happens, you feel it in your heart, and I don't feel anything.'[19]

President Peña Nieto, for his part, has warned that Mexico must not 'remain trapped' in the tragedy, and has urged its citizens to 'move on'. But the same lack of closure that has made it impossible for the parents to accept their sons are dead has kept the story alive. The Ayotzinapa case has not only brought unparalleled international attention to corruption, impunity and mass human-rights violations in Mexico, it has broadened protest into less radical sectors of Mexican society.

When R's parents arrived in Brisbane for our wedding in June 2015, my mother-in-law told me she'd stopped changing from one short course to another and had settled on a two-year diploma in thanatology – the scientific study of the needs of the dying and their families. Since there didn't seem to be a quiet corner of the country to retire to, they were planning to stay in the capital. They'd recently participated in several protests. Along with tens of thousands of ordinary Mexicans – not radicals, not revolutionaries – they had marched on the Zócalo.

Roraima & Manaus

Man's real home is not a house, but the Road.[1]
— Bruce Chatwin

Santa Elena came as a relief after Caracas: a dusty, industrious little outpost on the Venezuelan frontier where the major industries were black-market petrol, diamond mining and tourism. Massive queues of four-wheel drives often formed at the two petrol stations in town, where Brazilians filled up at prices thirty times cheaper than across the border. At a little tourist agency off the main road, Valentina and I joined a group of nine foreigners, all Europeans but for me, with whom we would make the six-day hike to the top of Roraima, a table mountain on the triple frontier between Venezuela, Brazil and Guyana.

'You're going to a very special place,' said the portly, lisping proprietor. He gave us each a world map marked with sites of supernatural energy. The lines connecting Stonehenge, the Bermuda Triangle, Machu Picchu and other 'mystic' places all intersected at Roraima.

'Some people see strange lights in the night sky,' he said. 'Some people experience an intense wave of sexual energy. Nobody leaves unchanged.'

He was a hard-headed businessman despite his mysticism. Asking around town, we learned that he kept prices low by underpaying the indigenous porters from the village of Paraitepuy who lugged tourists' camping and food supplies up the mountain. Many of them were only 14 or 15 years old. Since it wasn't possible to make the trek with another company that week, we told ourselves, with the adaptable self-righteousness of the young, that the only principled stand was to carry the equipment ourselves. In truth, we were both short of money – especially Valentina. As a result of our high-mindedness, we saved, and the agency still received our business. The porters got nothing.

Once on the move, we forgot our scruples with ruthless swiftness. We staggered out of town with 15 or 20 kilograms on our backs, like penitents in the Easter parades. For me, the ache of legs and arms brought a sense of plenitude and contentment. It felt good to be pushed physically and to burn off energy after a fortnight cooped up in the capital.

For the first two days, we walked through undulating savannah country, the mountain ahead of us mostly wreathed in cloud. We made a couple of river crossings in fast-flowing, waist-high water, our shoes dangling by their laces from our packs, the stones slick and mossy beneath our feet. The water was sweet and clear and perfectly safe to drink. In the afternoons, I would arrive into camp an hour or two ahead of the mostly middle-aged group and would roam about in search of pink mountain orchids, or dash off three or four dreadful poems in my journal before pitching the tent. The simple hearty meals of pasta, bread and beans prepared by our Guyanese guide, Alex, were so delicious that I gobbled double portions and finished off others' leftovers.

I was in awe of Alex. He was about 40 – which seemed old to me then – but was fitter than any of us. He carried enough weight for three people, and was equally comfortable categorising native bromeliads in English, Spanish and Portuguese. When everyone else was popping their blisters and moaning at the end of the day, he single-handedly cooked dinner for ten, refusing even to let us wash up. He had climbed the mountain more than 100 times. Watching how hard he worked, I began to suspect there were deep reserves inside me that I'd rarely tapped. And I started to understand the question the journey was posing: what was I going to do with that energy?

One day, when Alex and I were briefly marching alone at the front of the group, I asked him why he worked so hard.

'You must get good tips. What are you saving towards?'

He was putting money aside to send his three sons abroad. 'I don't want them carrying other people's shit down the mountain.'

He meant this literally. Park regulations dictated that human waste could not be left on top of Roraima. After the nearly 3-kilometre ascent to the summit on day three, we were supposed to defecate in a portable pot that would be carried back to town by the teenage porters.

For two days, I held on out of shame.

By the middle of the trek, poor Valentina had begun to struggle under the weight of her baggage.

'If I take the saucepan and your bed roll, will you stop whingeing?' I snarled, impatient to scale the mountain. Snatching the gear from her load, I ditched her at the back of the group, and made the ascent with Lena, a German PR consultant in her mid-thirties. A long-legged, athletic blonde with a ponytail, she was halfway through a round-the-world trip with her Irish boyfriend.

'He's been carrying a ring around at the bottom of his toiletries bag. I found it in India when I was looking for the Maxolon. He's going to propose at the top of the mountain, I know it.'

'That's good, isn't it?'

She looked down the rocky, near vertical slope and then upwards into the mist.

'I don't think he's the one.'

The afternoon we finally made the summit, the clouds were so thick we couldn't see a thing. In drizzling rain, we pitched our tents under a rock ledge amid prehistoric ferns and spiny yellow flowers. That night, in high spirits after the climb, we played an old parlour game around the campfire. Every member of the party had to tell two stories. The rest had to guess which was real and which was invented. It was not true, we discovered, that Anton, our companion from the Czech Republic, had discovered a Second World War grenade in his father's possessions when he was a boy. But it was true that he used to hitchhike between small-town beer halls in the old Czechoslovakia with his guitar, extending folk songs to 15 or 20 minutes to prolong his time in the warmth.

Soon, Irish William rose to take his turn. He was a skinny, cauliflower-eared redhead, punching well above his weight with Lena.

'My first contention – and you can doubt me if you like – is that I managed to travel in India from January through March this year without getting a single case of the runs.'

He paused, taking a deep breath of clean mountain air into his lungs.

'My second contention is that over there in our tent, stashed with my toothbrush and dental floss, I have a 14-carat, white-gold engagement ring with a big, fuck-off diamond in it. And tonight, when we go to bed, I'm gonna ask Lena to be my wife.'

Next morning, we woke with blue skies above, boiling clouds below. We basked like lizards on the sun-warmed stone, peering down through gaps in the low-hanging cumulus: rolling grasslands to the north and south, dense jungle to the east. At that place, in that moment, there seemed to be no limit to the shining earth, or to the people you could be in a lifetime. 'Brazil' was painted on a cairn of pebbles, an arrow pointing due south.

'We're headed into the Amazon,' I said to Valentina. 'Can you believe it?'

'I can't believe we have to walk all the way back.'

The mountain-top euphoria wasn't working for her. She was worn out from carrying so much weight. Nearby, Lena and Anton were excitedly grilling Alex about the geology of the rock formations.

'Besides, I can't stop thinking about that poor Irish boy,' said Valentina. 'Look at him.'

William sat on his own very near the cliff's edge.

We disembarked from the bus just south of Santa Elena, in the little town of Pacaraima, better known as 'the Line'. Here, the Venezuelan and Brazilian flags flew side by side, with a bust of Simón Bolívar to the north and of Don Pedro I to the south. The border officials spoke Portuñol, an improvised amalgam of Spanish and Portuguese. They were more concerned with the long queue of trucks transporting cargo across the border than a pair of down-at-heel foreigners. With a minimum of fuss, they checked our visas and yellow-fever vaccination certificates, and told us the quickest way to cross was to simply walk along the road's edge, past the banked-up vehicles. The idea of walking across the border appealed to me enormously: the slow pace, the smallness of the human form in the vastness of America, the impression – not so obvious in a bus or plane – that there is no line, really, that our divisions are invented, arbitrary, recent.

I was reading more Bruce Chatwin than was good for me in those days and I'd mistaken a great raconteur and yarn-spinner for a thinker. On the basis of his travels and his amateur anthropological study of nomadic cultures, Chatwin rejected the notion humans are naturally violent. He claimed weapons had only been developed as protection against ancient predators and were turned against other humans due to the stagnation of life in farms and cities. His solution to modern civilisation's woes was a return to permanent movement: the 'nomadic alternative'. Four months in, I was having my doubts. It was beginning to look more like a rationalisation of Chatwin's personal wanderlust than a viable life philosophy. Without family, community, a lover, a home to retreat to, I felt unmoored.

'Don't you ever miss home?' I asked Valentina as we lined up for our entry stamps at Brazilian customs. 'Don't you ever miss your family?'

'My father has a young baby with his second wife. He doesn't have time for me. My mother just wants me to be a schoolteacher. To get married and be boring. My brother is in a very expensive mental hospital. Personally, I'd rather spend my money on bus tickets.'

We lugged our packs across the spongy grass at the roadside.

'I was a teacher, back in Australia. I had a job teaching English to refugees.'

I told her about Roy, one of my Sudanese students in Brisbane. Walking across borders held no romance for him. When we'd sat together at a computer and looked up a map of Africa, he didn't want to retrace the vast wilderness of his homeland that he'd traversed on foot or revisit the borders he'd crossed. He wanted to locate the camp where he'd found safety and zoom in on one particular rooftop.

'That one. That is my hut. I built it with my hands.'

Valentina and I barely spoke during the 1000-kilometre bus trip south. With her language notebook in her lap, she mouthed Portuguese words like a spell against thoughts of home while I watched the grasslands bake in the hard sunlight for so long I felt as if the landscape was flowing through me. 'The sky looks big where there are no build-ings,' I wrote in my journal. Then, towering trees swallowed the highway.

Manaus, the jungle metropolis: 2.5 million people at the centre of the largest forest on earth. Here, the sandy-coloured upper river, the Solimões, converges with the dark Rio Negro to form the Amazon, and squirrel monkeys scamper along the powerlines. Still buzzing from the journey, I spent a blissful afternoon alone on the terrace of our hotel, drinking beer in the sun, and strumming Dylan's 'Chimes of

Freedom' on the yellow nylon-string guitar I'd bought at the markets for 300 reales. Brightly coloured laundry fluttered on rooftops across town, and huge ocean liners approached the port from the direction of the Atlantic, more than 1500 kilometres to the east. Valentina was arranging our passage on a smaller boat, a jungle cargo ship, that would take us five days down the Madeira River to the Bolivian border, where we would cross over and inch our way back from the deep Amazon to the Andes.

She crashed out early that night, weary from walking all day in the stifling equatorial heat. A little after eight o'clock I stumbled from the hotel, drunk and hungry, to search for dinner. Thunder grumbled in the distance; the air thickened like soup. Sunday night. Many of the places in our immediate neighbourhood were closed. I passed up a couple of well-lit, expensive-looking family restaurants because I didn't feel like sitting alone at a table.

The downpour caught me wandering, disoriented in a strange neighbourhood. Torrential rain clattered machinegun-fierce on metal rooftops. Taking shelter beneath an awning, I recognised William from the trek locked in a tight embrace with a Brazilian woman in a short skirt. A bottle of cachaça was open on the ground between them, and sweat poured from their bodies; they seemed to be trying to eat each other's faces. As he lifted his watery blue eyes, recognising me over her shoulder, he shot me a look of shame and hatred that sent me lurching into the warm rain. All along the avenue, sex workers in doorways hissed at me as I passed, dripping, singing 'Chimes of Freedom' softly to myself, letting myself be drenched. I wanted the same thing William wanted, I realised, but couldn't – not ever – for no reason I could articulate.

After nearly an hour, I stumbled upon Manaus's magnificent Belle Époque opera house, floodlit and gleaming like a pink gemstone. I'd read it was built during the rubber boom of the 1880s with Italian marble, English steel and French roof tiles. Distant strings and trumpets lured me into the lobby, where I caught a glimpse of my wild beard and matted hair reflected in the ticket seller's plexiglass screen.

'*Não há bilhetes*,' said the clerk, looking me up and down. No tickets left.

More magnificent even than the opera house was the sight of the barbeque stand just across the street. Two men in t-shirts and thongs sheltered beneath a large umbrella, chatting with the stall owner as he cooked meat skewers over glowing coals.

'Give me five of those...no, six,' I said, squeezing beneath the umbrella.

The other two customers fell silent, munching their dinner.

'*Que musica é?*' I asked, pointing at the opera house.

'E-vag-ner,' said one of the men, speaking with his mouth full.

'Wagner?'

And that much was true. I recognised the theme. They were playing 'Ride of the Valkyries' in the Amazon.

'We're in the chorus,' said the other man, gnawing away. 'We don't come on until the second half.'

I laughed so hard at that, I found I couldn't stop. I had to wipe my nose clean on my bare wrist.

'Would you sing for me? I've come from very far away and I can't afford a ticket.'

Bless those two perfidious Amazonians, they made a lonesome traveller very happy. They flung their wooden skewers on the ground, wiped their chins clean and sang for me, there beneath the umbrella in the pouring rain. They were no opera singers. From across the plaza, a stray dog barked along with their tone-deaf butchery of the Brazilian anthem. All four of us laughed, even the stall owner.

'*De onde você é?*' asked the second tenor, giggling.

'Brisbane.'

'*Onde?*'

'Queensland.'

'*Onde?*'

'Australia.'

'*Aus-tralia?* What are you doing here?'

That was a good question. It was what Rimbaud asked himself in Abyssinia, and Bruce Chatwin asked himself from London to Tierra del Fuego to the outback. I still didn't have an answer. All I could say, upon considered reflection, was: 'I have absolutely no idea.'

But at least I had found the question.

Don't Care if It Ever Rains Again

I had my own land once
children, cattle, and a woman,
but my suffering began,
they cast me out to the frontier —
and what did I find on my return?
A ruin, nothing more.[1]

— José Hernández, *Martín Fierro*

The *Spirit of the Outback* inched from Roma Street Station into the moonlight. In the sudden darkness, the train on the adjacent line peeled off to the right, carving a curved course into the suburbs. A rattle, a thump, and we accelerated in the opposite direction. Since returning from Argentina, I'd taken to exploring my home state like a foreign country, making long train and bus trips into unknown towns of the interior. I'd pitch my two-person tent away from the grey nomads and backpackers and lie awake on the hard earth listening to cicadas whir. There were no travel agents to tempt me in those little Queensland towns, and I was beyond the reach of Skype calls. But my thoughts still turned and turned to a certain dark-haired psychology major on the pampa. To distract me on the overnight train, I'd brought *Martín Fierro*, Argentina's nineteenth-century epic about a gaucho driven from his land into a life of crime.

I woke to see a scrapyard glinting in early daylight. By the tracks, abandoned sleepers were piled upon the stony red-black earth. A shredded tyre hung from a post near the highway and, beyond it, crooked wire fences divided plains of wind-rippled yellow Mitchell grass. The horizon was smoky, the sky that glassy, cloudless blue that makes you think it will never rain again. But just outside of Barcaldine, the parched country turned green.

Barcaldine is 1500 people, 700 kilometres from the sea: a grid of streets over an artesian basin at the intersection of two highways. The Capricorn starts near Rockhampton in the east and runs along the northern edge of town; the Landsborough comes from the south, the direction of Tambo and Blackall, and hems the town in from the west. There are six pubs along the main street: the Railway, the Union, the Artesian, the Commercial, the Shakespeare and the Globe. I gazed into their dark interiors, breathing in the reek of beer and steak as I lugged my pack along the roadside past utes and four-wheel drives parked in red gravel. Near the white, wooden railway station, a fountain ran on artesian water pumped from the subterranean lake below. The skyline was dominated by a massive corrugated water tank, a windmill and the big-top tent of the Australian Workers Heritage Centre, a museum set up by the Hawke government to mark the 1991 centenary of the Queensland Shearers' Strike.

The Tree of Knowledge, the 200-year-old ghost gum under which the strike leaders once gathered, was missing when I visited in 2008. It had been poisoned by vandals two years earlier. A sign said the trunk was being preserved in a Department of Primary Industries laboratory and described the monument proposed for the site: the mummified stump beneath an artificial canopy. I could only laugh to think I'd travelled this far without sighting so much as the Stump of Knowledge.

Undeterred, I hiked out to the old fairgrounds on the north side of town, pitched my tent where there was no one else around. Pink-faced galahs squabbled over berries in bushes hung with purple blossoms. Huge white grasshoppers sprung about in spiky knee-length grass. I found a place in the shade of a very old, very beautiful blue gum. It wasn't the eucalypt I'd come to see, but what difference did it make? Any tree could be the Tree of Knowledge, I figured, if you sat beneath it long enough. I took out a sheaf of papers copied from the library archives and read William Lane, in 1893, imploring Australian workers to join him in Paraguay:

> Let we, who have the strength and courage and can get the means, go out into the wilderness and, forsaking all other things, live in the right way as an example to those who have no faith. And our happiness will be to the wretched as a guiding star.[2]

For a few minutes, I banished all thought of Argentina.

He boarded the train with me in Barcaldine – a weather-beaten face beneath a slouch hat, something squirming in the breast pocket of his blue-and-black checked shirt.

'What you got there, Jack?' the ticket collector asked.

'Ain't none of your concern.'

He threw himself down beside me, knocking my elbow so I dropped my book.

'Scuse me.' He winked and, leaning forward, offered me a peek into his pocket at the beady-eyed chick he was smuggling down to Brisbane. His long, bony fingers placed a kernel of corn in its beak.

'Present for my grandson,' he said as the train shunted away from the platform. 'You from Brissy?'

I nodded, tried to go back to *Martín Fierro*.

'What brings you out here?'

'I wanted to see the Tree...'

'The Tree of Knowledge? They poisoned it a couple of years back.'

'I know. I hear they're turning the stump into a statue.'

'Long way to come to see a stump.'

Jack's mouth didn't stop moving all day. Through Alpha, Emerald and Blackwater, past cattle cars, trainloads of coal bound for port, homesteads in the shimmering heat, he talked on and on, until the railroad turned east at Rockhampton, night fell and we were headed home.

'I lost everything in the nineties. Fifteen-hundred hectare of Mitchell country out on the Downs, six thousand head of cattle. My brother took the old man's land, my wife took the three boys. Now all I've got is an old caravan outside Barcy. It isn't surviving on the pension that gets to me; when money's low, I can always hunt roos.

'What gets to me is Mark having the run of the farm.

'Every year, I fly west for a few months to clear the murdering thoughts from my head. I do odd jobs for the blackfellas, up near The Hedland. Headed over there now, after I see my grandkids in Brissy. If the blackfellas have money, they pay. If they don't, they share their tucker. Dole cheques come on Thursdays so there's always trouble that night. They'll all swear at each other and start fighting.

'Jo Jo's been in prison again for knocking his wife about. Have a look at this.'

He whisked a pocket watch from his bundle in the rack over the aisle. Cracked glass and faded copper casing.

'Present to celebrate him getting out. We're going to fix water towers together. Fixing water towers been a speciality of mine these last years. I'll have to pick up my rifle at the police station so we can get some tucker. Last time I was out west they wouldn't let me buy bullets on account of little Johnny's gun laws.

'"You after a rifle?" asks the shopkeeper.

'"No, I only want bullets."

'"What do you want bullets for if you haven't got a rifle?"

'"I have got a rifle."

'"Show me your licence and I'll sell you your bullets."

'"It's a Queensland licence."

'"Then you've got an unlicensed weapon."

'"Licensed in Queensland."

'"I think you'd better go to the police."

'Down the station there's an old black lady in front of me trying to register her rifle. The officer, young city fella, already been with her half an hour, and he's rolling his eyes and puffing out his cheeks.

'"Says she can't see. Not gonna shoot much, is she?" That young cop's eyes are worse than hers.

'"She can't read, you bugger. Here, I'll fill it in for her."

'"Can't let you do that, I'm afraid."

'So old Auntie leaves hungry and the Law prevails.

'When my turn comes, he tells me I should have registered the gun before I arrived in WA. "You register now, I'll have to put it in storage for six months. You'll have to pay a fee. Otherwise, you got a week to take it back to Queensland."

'"Bugger it, I'll register," I say, and the young cop starts reading from the form. Probably thinks I can't read either.

'"Sporting? Recreation? Destruction of vermin?"

'"Food," I say. "How's a man supposed to get fed?"

'I'll have to pick the rifle up before I meet Jo Jo. Can't rely on the government to feed you nowadays. It's every bugger for himself.

'Can't even trust your own brother. Few months before the court kicks me off the farm, Mark sends me out to fix the water tower. The two of us co-managed the property after Dad died. A fifty-fifty split like he wrote in his testament. Dunno how many times I insisted we give Dad a proper headstone under the bloodwood. But Mark reckoned a bushman's unmarked grave suited the old man fine. He kept making changes round the property without my permission. Even cut down four-hundred-year-old trees that been standing on this country longer than white men, the ones we played under when we were boys. "Improvements round the property," he called it. Fixing the water tower was his next project. But he was too cheap to pay a tradesman.

'Me and my oldest boy climb the tower early morning before the day gets hot. One minute, Paul's plugging a hole in the side of the tank, the next he's jerking back and forward like a kid with palsy. I grab hold of him and

I start jerking, too, a sound coming off us like when you throw bacon in an oiled pan and it's real hot and sizzling and squirting up. I wake on the ground with Paul kneeling over. He's all right. I'm all right. A neighbour's there, and the paramedics, but no sign of Mark.

'"You been electrocuted," said the neighbour. "Doesn't look like an accident to me."

'After that I'm three weeks in hospital. They stitch my tongue up and put a metal rod in my back. Never been the same. Fell on a steel pipe. No one will give me a proper job the speed I work now. Only Jo Jo and his mates up near The Hedland, who aren't in any hurry. Mark never come see me in hospital. Only the neighbour shows up.

'"I'm off hunting in Alaska for the season," says he. "They pay you thirty K a month to shoot bear and moose. Maybe you want to try it when you're back on your feet?"

'When he leaves, I stare at his empty chair, thinking how much I'd like to shoot me a plain old rat.'

Jack and I sat in the bar as the train rattled through deep night. All the other passengers had retired to their seats. A sickle-shaped moon hung over the dark fields, shuddering with every bump in the rails. My elbows stuck to the tabletop from all the beer we'd slopped. The bartender cleared his throat.

'Well, fellas…'

Returning to my seat after pissing, I looked at the other passengers' faces upturned in the moonlight. Jack slept with his hat on and his mouth open; he was as foreign to me as any Argentine or Bolivian. Beyond the window, smudged distances and slumbering earth. I would have loved to sleep with that vast, raw country rolling by. But as soon as I sat down, he woke. And as soon as he woke, he started talking.

'Wasn't my intention to make trouble. We only went back to the farm to pick up a stack of fencing wire. That old judge wouldn't believe me, but it's true. The rifle was just a precaution.

'I'm loading the coil of wire into the back of the truck when Mark's ute comes rolling down the track towards us. He doesn't know what to say, just sits there with the window down and the motor idling. We watch a pair of crows in the road picking at the remains of a flattened roo.

'"You reckon we're gonna get any rain?" says Mark.

'"I don't care if it ever rains again."

'I sit the barrel of the rifle on the window ledge. He won't meet my eye. He's staring at squashed bugs on the windshield, gulping saliva like emu ale. That's a confession, far as I'm concerned.

'"You're trespassing on my property."

'"My old man's buried on this property."

'Mark slips his truck into gear.

'"If you come here again, I'll dig him up and throw him at you."

'The bullet passes within an inch of his nose. It sails clear out the window on the other side. Don't know if I meant to hit him or meant to miss. Behind me, Paul's arms are folded and his eyes are wide. He's shivering though it's noon and high summer. That's when I lost him, I guess, and his mum and John and Michael, too. He looks at me like I'm already in jail. And that gets me thinking a life sentence is a long time. I pull my rifle from the cabin and thump on the driver's side door. Mark spins his wheels in the gravel and the truck's off up the track, trailing dust. I open the cartridge, pour the bullets in the dirt. As I pass Paul the gun, his hands are shaking.

'"You reckon I did the right thing?"'

'He doesn't talk to me all the way home.'

Daylight. Suburban streets, traffic lights, car horns. We were approaching Roma Street Station. Passengers rose, yawning around us to haul their luggage from the overhead storage. We'd out-talked the night.

'Wasn't long after I lost the farm that I met Jo Jo and his wife at church in Rockhampton. First time I been in years. They're real religious up that way: Seventh Day Adventists. Place is always full of Islanders singing in big booming voices. The Samoan priest says: "Praise the Lord! Anyone want to repent?"

'Jo Jo gets up: "They just let me out of Capricornia Correctional after two years. I'm not gonna drink no more or knock my wife about."

'"Praise the Lord! Anyone else?"

'I figure I'd better get up. I can still see the fear in Paul's eyes and smell the powder.

'"I hear there's this fella named the devil," I tell the Samoan priest and his congregation. "I always figured I'd punch him between the eyes if I saw him. But then I hear there's this other fella named the Lord. I dunno what I'll do if I ever see him. Anyway, here's a song."

'I sing them "Ode to Joy" because I figure singing is repenting. But my voice is creaky compared to all those Islanders and I lose the tune. They all start laughing. The Samoan priest pats me on the back, a big grin on his face.

'"Praise the Lord," he says.

'"Praise the Lord," I say, and I sit down, and that's the repenting done.

'Jo Jo was off to see his mob out west.

'"Any water towers need fixing out there?"

'"Maybe, brother."

'And that's how I started going up The Hedland.'

On the platform, we mingled with starched and perfumed Brisbane office workers: eyes on their phones, headphones in their ears. Beside me in his slouch hat, a bag slung over his shoulder, Jack checked on the chick in his pocket – still going strong. He shook my hand with iron force, began to move away into the crowd.

'Thanks for listening to an old fella.'

'See you again some time.'

'You will: upstairs.' He jabbed a lean index finger at the unrelenting blue sky. 'I'll be there long before you are.'

On the bus trip to the western suburbs my head throbbed from lack of sleep. Thoughts of the girl from the Argentine pampa flowed into the vacuum Jack had left. It would take more than a train trip to dislodge her. Hungrily, I returned to *Martín Fierro*, pushing past the strangeness – the archaisms, the rhyming eight-syllable lines – to a perfectly familiar mythology: poor white men tending rich white men's cattle on stolen land. At the end of part one, Martín Fierro and his accomplice Cruz flee as fugitives to survive on the pampa with the Mapuche. I pictured them as Jack and Jo Jo, riding out from Port Hedland:

and soon, without being detected,
they crossed the frontier.
On the far side,
one clear morning,
Cruz told him to look back
at the last settlements
and two big tears
rolled down Martín Fierro's face.
And following their true course
they entered the desert.[3]

And the Village Was
Fair to Look upon

*Australia…knows so little of other lands, and perhaps less of South
America than she does of countries obviously not so much in natural
fellowship with her as her sister continent.*[1]

– Mary Gilmore

San Miguel del Monte is a pretty little town on the edge
of the Argentine pampa: all potholed streets and lowset,
white-washed houses. To the east, a freshwater lake; in every
other direction, the plains. Ten years ago, I lived there for
six months. What does it say about me that I remember
Monte more vividly than Macchu Picchu or the Pyramid
of the Sun? Mangy dogs roam about barking, kids ride
motorcycles too fast, farmhands in gumboots and berets
talk soy prices on the broken pavement. Though it's only
two hours south-west of Buenos Aires, most Porteños have
never heard of Monte. The town's one claim to fame is
historical. The nineteenth-century *caudillo* Juan Manuel de
Rosas kept his ranch nearby. As Governor of Buenos Aires
from 1829 to 1852, Rosas oversaw a reign of terror enforced
by secret police and assassinations of opponents, but also
imposed a fragile peace after a series of civil wars. In 1987,
authorities loaded his decaying ranch onto a truck, and

transported it 70 kilometres into Monte where, now restored, it enjoys pride of place in the plaza, and still sparks passionate arguments between Rosas' supporters and detractors. It's probably untrue that the building's distinctive pinkish-red hue, the colour of Argentine federalism, was produced by blending milk and cow's blood. But it's a good story to tell the tourists from the capital who rent the lakeside cabins in the warm months.

In the long, slow, spring afternoons, Leonard Barton and I would sit on the back porch of his house on the highest piece of land by the lagoon. Leonard was less interested in Monte's place in frontier mythology than the history of Argentina's English-speaking community. We ate apple pie rather than dulce de leche, drank Earl Grey in place of mate, and talked for many hours in our shared native tongue. 'I like to go back and find out how things started,' he often said. Despite a six-decade age gap, we struck up a friendship: trading English books and discussing them, slowly making our way through his best bottle of cognac. He told me tall stories about the origins of ballpoint pens, police fingerprinting and the crescent moon–shaped croissants – *medialunas* – that are an Argentine breakfast staple. But it was the story of his family origins that kept me coming. I thought there might be a book in it.

The son of an English father and an Australian mother, Leonard was born in Argentina in 1926, and was brought up within the close-knit Anglo-Argentine community of that era. Tall, blond-haired and blue-eyed, he looked and sounded English. 'You had to keep British because you were the superior race,' he told me. 'You'll never understand that because you never lived it. It was like a religion, Britishness.' At his school in Buenos Aires province in the 1930s and 1940s, Spanish was taught two hours a day like any other subject. It was a case of 'when in Rome, do as at home'. Leonard's notion of Britishness dated from the days when Argentina had the largest Anglo population outside the Empire and was affectionally known as the Sixth Dominion. In fact, he'd only visited the UK once, in the 1930s, during the Depression. He told me he watched the BBC to keep his English 'up to date'.

During my first week teaching English at the local agricultural college, Leonard issued an invitation through one of his wife Susanna's private language students. Word had reached him that an Australian was in town.

'Mr Barton is English,' said the student, 'but his grand-parents were Australians, so he'd like to meet you.' She showed me a book, Leonard's prized copy of *A Peculiar People: William Lane's Australian Utopians in Paraguay* by Gavin Souter.

'You don't have to come,' she said. 'He's a little crazy. If you let him, he'll tell you stories all day.'

Leonard's grandparents left Australia for Paraguay on 16 July 1893. That day, the official vessel of the New Australia Co-operative Settlement Association, the *Royal Tar*, sailed from Sydney Harbour, carrying 220 adult Australians and their children across the Pacific in search of a better life. The *National Advocate* poured scorn upon the expedition:

> On the assumption that life among wild oranges and *yerba mate* scrub has capabilities which it does not offer

in Australia, one of the most feather headed expeditions ever conceived since Ponce de León started out to find the Fountain of Eternal Youth, or Sir Galahad pursued the Holy Grail, is actually about to set forth.[2]

'Australia,' retorted the emigrants, 'is not the world. The Labor question is a world-wide question…we can best help our fellow-workers here by showing them what can be accomplished, by having faith in each other, and courage enough to try it.'[3] Eventually, more than 500 people had the courage to try Paraguay. Leonard's grandparents, Thomas and Margaret O'Donnell, were among them.

Thomas had emigrated from Ireland to Queensland in his teens and taken work as a shearer. At 25, he found Margaret Egan, 'a mere girl at the time', in a Barcaldine orphanage, where she'd lived since both parents had died in search of gold in the bush. 'Love is blind, marriage is an eye opener,' she told her grandson. Margaret was 15 when she gave birth to her first child. And Leonard's mother, Mary Ann, was only three when industrial strife broke out in Queensland. It would soon drive her parents from the country.

Like Monte, the central Queensland town of Barcaldine is best known for what happened there in the nineteenth century. Legend has it the Australian Labor Party was founded beneath a straggly ghost gum next to Barcaldine train station during the 1891 Queensland Shearers' Strike. The strike was triggered by a downturn in the global wool market. When pastoralists tried to pass losses on to their workers – proposing tougher working conditions and demanding freedom of contract – the workers responded by setting up and maintaining strike camps in rural centres for nearly six months. The largest was at Barcaldine. At the height of the conflict, some 10,000 shearers and station hands lived in the camps, with 800 rifles at their disposal. The colonial government put down the strike through a show of overwhelming force designed to deter similar industrial action elsewhere in Australia. They sent in 1400 well-armed troops and jailed all but two of the 14 strike leaders in harsh conditions on the prison island of St Helena, off Brisbane. This crushing defeat for organised labour accelerated the push for working-class parliamentary representation that culminated, in 1904, with the election of the first labour government anywhere in the world. It also provided the impetus for the New Australians' radical Paraguayan experiment.

The leader of the movement was the charismatic British-born journalist William Lane. Lane placed advertisements in union newspapers like *The Worker* and *The Boomerang*, asking would-be members to surrender their life savings to the organisation, to a minimum commitment of £60. Leonard's grandfather, 'fed up with the situation in Australia', threw in his lot with the Utopians.

Before the O'Donnells were halfway across the Pacific, cracks had begun to appear in the colonists' facade of revolutionary comradery. Seasickness, boredom and infighting affected morale during the two-month journey. Margaret O'Donnell recalled to her grandson that William Lane prohibited her and the other young mothers from buying treacle for their children. Treacle was made from molasses, and rum came from molasses – violating Lane's strict alcohol ban. Scandalised by a romance between two crew members, Lane banned unmarried women on deck after dark, prompting an immediate backlash. Later, there was near mutiny over the loss and ensuing scarcity of cutlery. So fragile is Utopia it can be undone by a shortage of forks. By the time the *Tar* arrived in Paraguay, its occupants were divided into two factions, the royals, who remained loyal to Lane, and the rebels, who chafed at his autocratic ways.

Lane's brand of socialism was puritanical, religiously inflected, and deeply conservative. Many of his founding precepts proved impractical, especially the alcohol ban. Leonard's grandfather was a teetotaller but made a living in the days of the colony's decline selling *caña*, or sugar cane rum, to rebel colonists. It was made clear to members they were not to 'cross the colour line' by consorting with Paraguayans. Lane was a fanatical racist, even by the standards of the time. He hoped that the remoteness of the land they had been granted by the Paraguayan government would protect the colony from the pollution of external influences. In fact, it hampered trade that would have made their lives more comfortable.

The Paraguayans had offered a parcel of nearly 200,000 hectares of good-quality land in the country's south-east, between two branches of the Tebicuary River. Land grants to European immigrants were common at the time. The country was trying to rebuild after the War of the Triple Alliance (1864–1870), a prolonged and bloody conflict in which the small South American republic took on its powerful neighbours Brazil, Uruguay and Argentina, all at once. In the aftermath, missing an entire generation of working-age men, Paraguay offered free land to everyone from German Mennonites to Australian bushmen.

The New Australia colonists toiled hard and made some progress in the early days in Paraguay. They cleared 40 hectares of land, planted 20 hectares of crops, constructed makeshift dwellings, and built other essential buildings. Thomas O'Donnell started a tannery, dug pits for curing meat, built dams for the cattle, and ran a general store. Margaret, like many of the women who had made the journey out of obligation to their husbands rather than their own convictions, disliked the rough life in the colony.

By the end of the year, a third of the initial group had left New Australia. Many colonists complained they had been misled by the scouting party's report on the site, particularly regarding its proximity to the railway line and the river. Others found the rigours of communal living too much. They wanted to barter with the local Guaraní people, but didn't like the idea of contributing their profits to the public coffer. Some of the single men took a shine to *caña* and others became romantically involved with Paraguayan women. Lane brought tensions to a head by trying to expel the rebel leaders for breaking the temperance law. When the men refused to leave voluntarily, Lane called in the Paraguayan police and had his opponents forcibly removed. For many of the colonists, the scene of their comrades being dragged off by armed officers was reminiscent of Barcaldine days. The incident sparked a mass exodus from New Australia.

The colony lasted barely three years in its original form. As Gavin Souter observed: 'nothing ever quite came up to expectations – crops, industry, education, or human nature.'[4] Accusations of financial mismanagement were levelled at the leadership group; there were cattle rustlers from inside the colony; relations between the first batch of colonists and later arrivals were tense. Many of those who left the colony moved elsewhere in Paraguay or in South America, while others asked for financial assistance from the Australian, Paraguayan and Argentine governments, to help them return home.

In July 1894, William Lane left with his closest disciples to establish Cosme Colony on a second parcel of land 72 kilometres further south. The poet Mary Gilmore – a true believer in the cause and an intrepid traveller – paid her own passage and journeyed alone from Sydney by ship, paddle-steamer, train and on horseback to join Cosme.[5] Back at New Australia, the land was divided into private lots and shared between the few hardy souls who remained. Thomas O'Donnell was among them, but his wife was not. Like the colony itself, Thomas and Margaret's marriage disintegrated in Paraguay. 'When poverty comes in the door, love flies out the window,' Leonard recalled his grandmother saying. The O'Donnells lived apart for the best part of 30 years in old age, but not before having nine children who would grow up in South America and have their own families.

I visited the village of Nueva Londres, on the site of the old Australian socialist colony in central southern Paraguay, in August 2008. It was a long, rough bus journey, even in the twenty-first century: 1400 kilometres from Buenos Aires. At the border town of Encarnación, on the Paraguayan side of the Paraná River, nobody had heard of the village. After making a couple of phone calls, a ticket seller at the bus station informed me I'd need to travel to a junction in the highway named 'Kilometre Thirty' then catch a connection to Coronel Oviedo, the closest town to the settlement.

With the first bus departing at two in the afternoon, I assumed I'd have plenty of daylight to make the connection and find accommodation. But poor visibility and road conditions meant we didn't complete the first leg until well after dark. A wild thunderstorm battered the bus, lighting up the grasslands and the thick, sucking red mud at the roadside. Passengers disembarked at an endless series of drop-offs. Kilometre Thirty was little more than two tin-roofed shelters on either side of the highway. Near where I was dropped off, a large group of rough-looking truckers glared at me, drinking the famous *caña*. As I retreated, a young indigenous woman with a strangely inexpressive face grabbed hold of my arm. The downpour and unexpected appearance of a green-eyed foreigner had triggered something in her. She clung to me across the swampy dirt highway, keening and sobbing at the top of her lungs until I extricated myself and slithered away. I will never forget the sight of her howling in the deluge. The ticket vendor loaded me onto an overcrowded bus and overcharged me. For three or four hours, I stood in the aisle drifting off on my feet, clinging to the overhead luggage rack. At Coronel Oviedo, I disembarked after midnight, found rough lodgings at a roadside inn, and crashed into bed without dinner.

I awoke sufficiently recovered to continue searching. Originally New Australia under William Lane's Utopians, the village became Colonia Stroessner during the reign of Paraguay's Cold War–era strongman and, after democracy returned in 1992, was finally renamed Nueva Londres (New London) by the new mayor, in honour of his own British heritage. I trudged past a chaotic array of fast-food

bars, kiosks and auto repair shops and finally encountered
the Coronel Oviedo bus station. There, I was told that the
colectivo to Nueva Londres would arrive at half past ten.
A little after eleven, I asked again, and was told it wasn't
running because of last night's rain. Soon, I found myself
clinging to the back of a Paraguayan taxi driver named
Alberto, who cautiously negotiated the traffic on Ruta 2 on
his little red Honda motorcycle and took the turn-off to
Nueva Londres. Excitement rippled through me as we passed
beneath the sign for the village, which I had seen in photos.
Finally, the sun was shining in Paraguay. Dew sparkled on
the pastures. Stands of dense *monte* scrub rose from the plains
at a distance from the highway, and we passed many straggly
groves of orange trees, a legacy of Jesuit missionaries in
the seventeenth and eighteenth centuries. Narrow, fast-
flowing streams snaked through the fields, and waist-high
red anthills dotted the plains. I remembered a passage from
Mary Gilmore's diaries describing owls sitting on the anthills
at sundown, eyes gleaming in the Paraguayan dusk.

About half an hour after we set out, Alberto dropped
me in the shady plaza at the centre of Nueva Londres. The
H-shaped monument was in such a bad state of repair that
most of the names etched into the metal were illegible. The
few I could make out were Spanish and didn't seem to have
any relation to the Australian colonists. As I walked around
the village, many of the street names were familiar from
my reading about the colony. The main road was the calle
Ricardo L. Smith. Cattle and horses wandered the fringes
of the settlement. Kids buzzed about on motorbikes. The
red-earth roads were rutted and muddy. Puddles reflected
the Paraguayan sky. The streets were mostly empty as the

hour of the siesta approached, but smoke was billowing from a backyard *parilla*. I could smell barbequed meat and hear somebody, far off, blowing a major scale on the trumpet. Because it was the weekend, the office of the municipal government was closed and it was not easy to work out who to talk to. A local teenager suggested I visit señora Iris Kennedy, who lived in the white house on the plaza in front of the school and would be able to tell me about the town's history. The boy told me I was the third Australian to blunder into the village that year. 'Every year four or five foreigners come.'

La señora Kennedy had hosted overseas visitors before. She ushered me into her living room and insisted, despite my protests, on serving me a glass of milk fresh from her family's own cows. She told me she still understood some English when she heard it, but that she wasn't able to speak the language. All the English speakers had died out, she told me in Spanish, even Don Eduardo, who for a long time hosted the bulk of Australian visitors. Now that role had fallen to her. I remembered that her uncle, Juan Kennedy, featured heavily in Anne Whitehead's account of the colony.[6] Iris Kennedy was a petite woman in her seventies, with lively, darting green eyes and white hair. She told me memory of the Australian colony was dying out in Nueva Londres.

'We are all Paraguayan now.'

The villagers were more concerned with present-day living conditions than the past. The bus service that had let me down apparently no longer runs at all, leaving local residents reliant on private vehicles, moto-taxis and a community minibus that intermittently ferries children to school in town. Iris Kennedy described how a younger relative used to leave to attend the nearest university in Villarrica at seven in the morning and return at eleven o'clock at night. When I asked for her address, she told me the postal service no longer operates.

She wasn't comfortable talking about the colony beyond the brief, rehearsed spiel that she gave when I first arrived. Paraguayans weren't interested in that part of their history, she insisted. 'We have no culture,' she kept saying. Iris said she hadn't been to school beyond the sixth grade, but she was extremely proud of her daughter, who had become a teacher at the local primary school. This, she told us, was the most Paraguayans could hope for: to work hard and to give their children a better life. The country had great hopes for the new president, she said. President Lugo, a progressive former priest, was the first Paraguayan leader in 60 years not from the conservative Colorado Party. But Paraguayans 'couldn't afford too much hope'. She was right about that. Five years later, President Lugo was impeached on dubious grounds and Colorado rule was restored.

As with Leonard Barton, one of the remaining signs of Iris's heritage was her cooking. She boasted of her repertoire of Australian and English recipes, including cakes, biscuits and brownies. Señora Kennedy remembered the name of Thomas O'Donnell, Leonard's grandfather, but she had never met him. After we'd chatted for an hour, she showed me the bananas, pears, peaches and chillies planted in her garden ('I just planted the chillies because I like the colour'). Not wishing to impose on her hospitality any further, I thanked her and took my leave.

There was no sign of Alberto, despite his solemn promise to return to the plaza and pick me up, so I walked

8 kilometres out of the colony through the gorgeous countryside, all the way back to the highway. I have rarely been happier than I was that day when I came upon a horse-drawn cart, old enough for me to imagine it might be a relic of the colony, abandoned on its side, in the lush Paraguayan grass. I sat beside it and puzzled over Thomas More's lovely sixteenth-century coinage. How could somewhere be both a good place and no place? I wondered that afternoon, on the road out of Nueva Londres, if it might be best to think of Utopia as temporal rather than spatial, a mental state rather than a physical location. In that case, instead of suggesting an unachievable ideal, it might imply a feeling all of us will experience – momentarily – in our lifetime. In the long grass at the roadside, eating an orange in drenching sunlight, I was there for a good half-hour.

Leonard's mother, Mary Ann, spent her childhood helping out in her father's general store in the colony. She and her sister Hanna wrote on the goods in secret code so they would know how much they were allowed to discount the price of each item. The two were forbidden to speak Guaraní, the local language, as it would 'make them familiar to the natives'. Both escaped the limited world of the colony through marriage, Hanna marrying an engineer, Bob Green, and Mary Ann an English railwayman, William Allan Barton.

Leonard's father began his time in South America working on the railway in Mendoza, at the foot of the Andes in north-west Argentina, until he and nearly 6000 others were fired for going on strike. After returning briefly to Buenos Aires, William set out in search of his fortune. In

Paraguay, on his way north to look for diamonds in Brazil, he found a wife instead. He had met Mary Ann's brother Tom in Asunción and was invited to celebrate Christmas at New Australia. The eligible bachelors of the British community in Paraguay often visited the colony in those days, in the hope of meeting single women. 'It was a lively thing,' Leonard said. The colonists put on theatrical productions, poetry recitals and dances, often accompanied by Paraguayan harp music. William and Mary Ann Barton met at one such gathering.

Leonard's older sister Aileen was born in Paraguay in 1917, but the family soon left for good. William was called to serve in the First World War, but only made it as far as Rosario in Argentina. 'The armistice got him,' said Leonard. His father returned to railway work, first in Rosario and later in Victoria, Buenos Aires province, where Leonard was born in 1926.

While Leonard only ever heard of New Australia through the stories of his grandmother and mother, his sister Aileen visited the former colony as a child. William and Mary Ann took Aileen to meet her grandfather at three years old, during a period of civil war in Paraguay. One night, Thomas O'Donnell saw troops approaching the colony. He hid his daughter and granddaughter under the bed, lowered all the alcohol down the well, and waited. When the soldiers arrived, they sacked his store, stole his cattle and tied him to a tree. By the time the Bartons departed the next day, all that remained was a box of matches and a sack of flour. It took Aileen and her parents six months to escape Paraguay and return home.

'There's a young Australian journalist here and I'm spilling all the dirt on the family,' Leonard told his older sister over the phone. Aileen Barton was in her nineties and lived in Buenos Aires but remained in regular contact with her younger brother. She didn't want to talk to me about the colony. 'She thinks it's shameful,' Leonard said. What did he think? Was New Australia really such a failure? Australian writers like Gavin Souter and Anne Whitehead have given the short-lived experiment near mythic status. 'Australia does not have many legends,' wrote Souter,

> but those it does have are all concerned with people who took their chances against great odds, and failed: Eureka, Cooper's Creek, Glenrowan and Gallipoli. The odds against Utopia were also great, none greater, and it seemed to me that New Australia and Cosme might be added to the list.[7]

Leonard was less sympathetic towards his ancestors' project. 'Absolutely it was a failure…They had a silly philosophy: if you were a schoolteacher you worked as a cobbler.'

His biography and political opinions showed little trace of his Irish grandfather's radicalism. After completing his military service in the 1940s, he was in textiles for some years. In the 1950s, he worked with British American Tobacco in Buenos Aires. Later, he would go into business keeping beehives. His own children and grandchildren spoke English, but hesitantly, as a second language, and had not inherited the 'religion' of Britishness. The closest Leonard came to socialism was a vague disapproval of the materialism of the younger generation. Nevertheless, while he was conservative in many of his views, I had the sense he was much too independent-minded, too much of a peculiar person, to adhere to any consistent ideology. 'I don't have much time for idealists,' he said, 'not at my age, but I think it's for the young people to be idealistic.'

Not long after returning from Paraguay, I visited the reading room of the John Oxley Library, which looks towards Brisbane city from the southern riverbank. With its shabby, outmoded skyscrapers and jacarandas in bloom beside the slow-moving brown water, my hometown now reminded me of subtropical river towns I'd visited in northern Argentina, like Rosario and Posadas. At the library, I skimmed through a near complete set of *Cosme Monthly*, the little journal published out of the second, longer-lived Australian colony in Paraguay between December 1894 and December 1900. Printed on rough yellow paper, it was distributed in England and Australia in the hope of gaining 'sufficiency of membership' for the struggling settlement.

The early editions, handwritten by hungry people and copied for distribution, abandon William Lane's lofty style for a frank assessment of the hardships of pioneer life. 'January 1894: Cash and food both short beginning of month; nearly reached bedrock. Got 1500 lbs beans on credit; ate beans till corn grew.'[8] By February 1897, however, the journal has shifted to printed text and Lane's familiar, fanatical tone returns to the anonymously authored articles: 'We Germanic peoples come into history as Communists. From our communal villages we drew the strength which broke Rome down.'[9] Disillusioned with increasing numbers of colonists abandoning Cosme, Lane resigned as chairman in 1899 and left for Auckland, where he ended his days as a lead writer for the conservative *New Zealand Herald*. Writing editorials as Tohunga – Maori for prophet – he criticised industrial lawlessness, argued for universal military service, and praised the cause of British imperialism. Lane, in the words of one union-aligned journal, 'died in the camp of the enemy'.[10]

After his departure, the editorship of *Cosme Monthly* presumably fell to Mary Gilmore, for the writing gains a refreshing feminine perspective and a felicity of style in the later issues. The single most poignant piece of writing about the Australians in Paraguay is an anonymously authored short story, 'A Cosme Dream' – surely the work of Gilmore – which was published in *Cosme Monthly* in March 1898 and, to my knowledge, has never been reprinted. Like the literary Utopias of the prominent socialist writers Edward Bellamy and William Morris which inspired many real-life experiments in the nineteenth century, the story is a dream of an ideal future. It is narrated by a Cosme pioneer who lies down to sleep at the end of a hard day's labour and is granted a brief vision of the community's magnificent future:

> Tired and worn with the toil of a hot summer's day, I lay on my bed, and, as the sun went down, slept. And in my sleep, suns rose and set, moons waxed and waned, and silent seasons passed swift-winged by like cloud shadows on the meadow. And when in my sleep I awoke, the earth had grown older by many years and lay unrolled to my curious eyes like a fairy picture. And as I looked, the sun

rose through a golden mist, and his golden beams glinted on cottage roofs, half-hid in groves of orange, palm, and fig. For a village was there spread out on a gentle rise that overlooked wide tree-dotted plains, where the morning mists made the grazing cattle like living shadows. And the village was fair to look upon.[11]

Redcliffe

I build a cairn of words over a silent man.[1]

– John Manifold

What was I doing in Latin America?

The richest decade in Australian history felt, to me, like a dismal time to be young. In 2006, I'd found myself back from Beijing, house-sitting for my parents in Brisbane's leafy western suburbs. I was older than my grandfather when he went to war, but only beginning to recognise my luck. Several afternoons a week my ESL teacher friends and I stayed in the city until late. We'd down jug after jug of Tooheys New at O'Malley's or Jimmy's on the Mall, or the old Criterion, where Malouf's Johnno and Dante used to drink. And we'd rage about the state of Howard's Australia while taking no action to change it: the republic as remote as Kafka's castle; the refusal to apologise to Indigenous Australians; the demonisation of the unemployed; the mining revenue wasted on welfare for fat rich people with six televisions tuned perennially to Channel Nine; 'one for Mum, one for Dad, one for the treasurer'; noxious cricketing metaphors poisoning public life; the refusal to sign Kyoto; the dog whistles on race – Hansonism, Cronulla; our obsequious participation in US wars; the cruelty, the sheer cruelty of our little Pacific gulag for boat people.

All these complaints, though sincere, were mostly a cipher for my self-disgust. I couldn't forgive myself for being brought up in the suburbs by my two loving parents on the forested rim of a safe and prosperous subtropical city. For having read too much and lived too little. I didn't want to read about life anymore; I wanted to go where life was happening. I didn't want peace and prosperity; I wanted to be cold and uncomfortable. I wanted to wear holes in my shoes, catch fever in unpronounceable places. I wanted to grow a beard, and call my mother from prison, and look like a Dostoevsky villain in the mugshot. I'd been heartbroken twice (I thought). Some good poems had come of it. I was hoping to try again.

It was high time I left for Latin America.

My parents were on sabbatical in Hong Kong that year, and my younger brother was on exchange in Kobe. If this was my milieu, by what right did I feel enraged? The absence of a clear cause only made it worse. Early each weekday, I caught the bus to Spring Hill, where I taught English to refugees and new migrants at a private college run by a robust, floral-bloused former school principal, who insisted our adult students refer to her as 'Mrs Sheridan'. Mrs Sheridan once confiscated a bilingual dictionary from a 70-year-old Chinese grandmother – new to my class and to the country – who didn't speak enough English to understand dictionaries were banned. Mrs Sheridan insisted teachers prepare lessons alone in their classrooms rather than fraternise in the staffroom.

'What is this? A union meeting?' she used to say, upon catching two colleagues conversing in the hall. She and her husband were generous and prominent donors to the Liberal Party. It was no coincidence, my colleagues said, that our school was the only private provider of language courses in Queensland to have a contract with the federal Immigration Department. Our students hailed from all corners of the earth, the youngest in their late teens, the oldest in their eighties. Most of the Europeans, Asians and South Americans had married Australians or were skilled migrants. They were older, worldlier and better educated than I was, with my Bachelor of Arts and dodgy English teaching certificate from China. They could see I was out of my depth with the refugee students and tried to help by suggesting activities and outings. Sometimes, kicking a football under the fig trees by the Brisbane River with those taciturn, unsmiling boys from Sudan, Eritrea, Burundi and the Congo, it was possible to imagine we'd arrived at a place beyond history. But in the classroom shattering stories came out at unexpected moments, not just from the Africans, but also from the Iraqis and Afghanis, who'd fled lands Australia had recently helped invade and was still occupying. Once, I set the intermediate class an innocuous exercise: 'Write ten sentences in the simple past tense. Underline the verb.' That night, marking the responses by lamplight in the cavernous silence of my parents' home, I encountered the phrase 'Bomb <u>killed</u> my mother, father, brother, sister, uncle.'

In the evenings, I cooked huge pastas and curries to last me for three or four days, and stayed up late, sampling my father's liquor cabinet, sometimes mapping curriculums and course plans I was unqualified to write, more often composing short stories that were always set in Beijing or Ulaanbaatar, never in Brisbane. I struggled to sleep and would drift off listening to the news from Iraq on the BBC World Service. By the mid-2000s, most of the school and university friends with whom I'd marched against the war were overseas or in the larger southern capitals. But I was back in Brisbane, the war was still going, and John Howard would be Prime Minister forever.

My maternal grandfather was my only family in Queensland that year. I always called him Al, an informal habit acquired from Mum. Every couple of weekends, I'd drive out to visit him on the Redcliffe peninsula, 40 minutes north of the city. We'd stroll the waterfront near the memorial for the original Moreton Bay penal colony and eat chocolate ice-cream, watching waves gently lapping the sand. Back in his two-bedroom villa, we'd crank Chopin or Sinatra so loud he didn't need his hearing aid. His house was decorated with my grandmother's old oil paintings of pastoral Victoria, competent imitations of the Heidelberg School. He liked to take down the dusty old atlas from his bookshelves – the USSR still marked in threatening crimson – to trace for me the route of the ship that took him to Europe in 1940. His one journey abroad. I knew even then that I ought to write the story of his childhood and war service: a record of his memories that wouldn't die with him. But it didn't seem urgent when I was 23. I was more interested in showing him the trip I was going to make in the new year when I'd saved enough money: 1200 kilometres across South America, from the Pacific coast of Ecuador to the Argentine River Plate.

'Why do you want to go there?' Al asked.

'I just do.'

Though he was a life-long Labor voter, I didn't think he'd approve of my interest in the new Latin American socialism, the plan to see for myself the countries of the so-called pink tide. And he certainly wouldn't have understood if I'd told him I wanted to learn Spanish so I could read García Márquez in the original.

In August, as the weather was warming up, one of my Beijing stories won a local literary award with prize money of a couple of thousand dollars. On seeing my picture in the *Courier Mail*, Mrs Sheridan called me to her office.

'We ought to be hanging on to a bright young fellow like you. We're making you permanent.'

It was the last offer of permanent employment I'd receive for a decade – everything, from then on, would be temporary. Al was delighted with the news.

'A permanent position!' he roared over the music when I told him that weekend. 'Congratulations!'

He poured us two glasses of flat ginger beer and proposed a toast. 'To full-time work.'

'I turned it down. I told them I'm quitting.'

'What? Why did you do that? I thought you liked it.'

He switched off the music. The ceiling fan whirred and the old wooden clock ticked and my grandfather wore a look of utter incomprehension, like the time I'd tried to explain the Internet.

'I like the students,' I said. 'But I hate my boss.'

'Well, have you at least got another job lined up?'

'No, I've got a plane ticket to South America in the new year.'

The oldest of six, Al had quit high school at 15 when his father died belatedly from being gassed during the

First World War. He supported his siblings and mother as a clerk at the gas and fuel company in Melbourne until joining the air force in the Second World War, and afterwards returned to the same company, where he remained for 25 years. My grandfather knew what Dresden looked like from above as it burned, and how it feels to be 20 years a widower. But the pleasure of throwing in a job just because you didn't like it was beyond him.

'What will you do in South America?'

'I don't really know. I'm going to study Spanish and read a lot. I guess I'll keep a journal on all the long bus trips.'

The ticket was already booked, the trip justified in my mind. I wasn't abandoning him. Mum and Dad would be back to keep him company by the time I left. His health was good and his mind was sharp. Writing the story of his war service could wait. There was no reason to believe he wouldn't be able to tell it when I came home: not if you were 23 and had never lost anyone.

Old Peak, Young Peak

I remembered the fields and stones, the squares and churches,
the streams where I had been happy.[1]

— José María Arguedas

'Jimmy! You made it,' Dad said, bursting into our suite on the eighth floor of the Lima Radisson. He let the door swing closed behind him, laid his laptop to one side, and enfolded me in a bear hug. The bristles of his beard pricked my cheek. As always, he seemed enormous to me: broad-shouldered, barrel-chested, overpowering. Perhaps his hair was a little greyer than when I last saw him, six months before, his beard a little whiter at the centre. He pulled back, clasping me by the shoulders, looking me up and down.

'You've lost weight, you skinny bugger.'

I saw in the floor-to-ceiling mirror that he was right. My 30th birthday present to myself, during the year R and I were separated, was a six-month backpacking odyssey through Spain and Central America between work contracts. I stopped replying to her emails in Salamanca, where I was supposed to be studying Spanish literature at the university. Instead, some classmates and I rented a black BMW and drove to Seville, the roof and windows open, screaming verses from Rubén Darío that Profesor Antonio had made us memorise: 'youth, divine treasure / now you are going never to return'.[2] With the trip about to end, I'd decided that it marked the conclusion of my career as a solo traveller. Too much drinking and not enough exercise had turned me into an inferior copy of Dad: the same wavy hair and square jaw, but gaunt, pale and round-shouldered.

'We'll have to fatten you up with those giant guinea pigs they eat here,' he said, hanging his jacket in the closet.

'How was your keynote?'

He rolled his eyes and groaned. 'They changed the venue at the last minute. Half the crowd went to the wrong place. The other half didn't speak English.'

Dad swished across the thick carpet in his socks and threw open the curtains. We were in the tallest building on the block, looking down on the gated barrio of Miraflores, all luxury hotels and flash restaurants behind high fences. I'd read somewhere that the function centre down the street, now hosting the seventh World Congress of Behavioural and Cognitive Therapies, had been bombed by Maoist guerillas in the early 1990s. Today, security guards patrolled the neighbourhood, and cameras surveyed the streets. Sky and city were an unvariegated grey. 'Donkey's belly grey', Limeños call it. A few blocks further west, cliffs fell away to a stony beach pounded by breakers. The Pacific. My ocean. Home lay that way.

Dad took a can of Cusqueña from the mini-bar fridge, cracked it, poured it into two glasses, and handed one to me.

'I'm trying to cut down on this stuff.'

'Have a beer with your old man.'

We lifted our glasses.
'To Machu Picchu.'

In his 1609 *Royal Commentaries of the Incas and General History of Peru*, Garcilaso de la Vega, the mestizo son of a Spanish conquistador and an Incan princess, recalls the story his uncle told him, as a boy, about the origins of the Inca kings:

> Nephew, I will tell you these things with pleasure: indeed, it is right that you should hear them and keep them in your heart...You should know that in olden times the whole of this region before you was covered with brush and heath, and people lived in those times like wild beasts, with no religion or government...Our father the Sun, seeing men in the state I have mentioned, took pity and was sorry for them, and sent from heaven to earth a son and a daughter of his to indoctrinate them in the knowledge of our father the Sun that they might worship him and adopt him as their god...With this order and mandate our father the Sun set these two children of his in Lake Titicaca, eighty leagues from here, and bade them go where they would, and wherever they stopped to eat or sleep to try to thrust into the ground a golden wand...when this wand should sink into the ground at a single thrust, there our father the Sun wished them to stop and set up their court.[3]

On our first night in Lima, Dad and I got smashed. It was something that occasionally happened when we found ourselves together without my mother's moderating influence. After our reunion at the hotel, we had dinner with Thomas, a psychology professor from Los Angeles, and his 18-year-old son, Ryan. The restaurant backed onto a 1500-year-old adobe and clay pyramid, Huaca Pucllana, which was floodlit after dark so that it glowed like a pile of stolen bullion. Dad ordered *ají de gallina*, and I ordered ceviche. We drank pisco sours with the entree, a crisp Chilean white with the main. The Americans drank water. Thomas and Dad discussed how important it was that their beloved Cognitive Behavioural Therapy was holding its biggest conference in Latin America, where psychoanalysis still reigned. Ryan, a pudgy kid with acne scars, hid behind his fringe and hardly spoke. I recognised my adolescent self in his slouching shyness, his tendency to let his father talk for both of them.

'Ryan's been studying Spanish since elementary school,' said Thomas. 'He's been helping me out with the lingo while we're down here.'

My father's colleague complimented my Spanish and asked where I'd learned.

'I've been wandering around Latin America for years now.'

Thomas took another piece of bread from the basket on the table. 'Don't get any ideas, Ryan. It's time you started college.'

'Have you chosen a major?' I asked.

'Not yet,' he mumbled.

Thomas chewed his potatoes thoughtfully. He swallowed and licked his lips. 'Psychology is under consideration.'

His son nodded, examining his placemat.

'It's a good option,' said Dad. When I scowled at him, he shrugged. 'Well, if he wants to.'

'You were never interested in the family trade, James?' asked Thomas.

'Not seriously. I was always more interested in fiction and poetry. Maybe that's another way of studying psychology.' I clapped Dad on the shoulder. 'Anyway, I knew I didn't want to live in this guy's shadow all my life.'

Ryan stared intently at the bread basket, and a long silence fell over the table, broken only by the smacking of lips.

Dad and I drank faster.

'Jimmy's a bit horrified that I've booked us onto a package tour in Cuzco,' he told them, speaking with his mouth full. 'He likes to organise everything independently. You know, saddle his own llama. But I thought since we have so little time...'

'Is this the three-day tour?' said Thomas. 'We did that last weekend. It was fantastic. I think you'll have half the conference there with you.'

'Imagine there's a landslide,' I said. 'Cognitive Behavioural Therapy could be wiped from the map.'

This was not as silly a suggestion as it sounded. In 2010, nearly 2000 visitors needed to be airlifted from Machu Picchu after heavy rain caused mudslides.

'Peru would be left to the psychoanalysts,' Dad said. 'Disastrous.'

Thomas pondered this possibility gravely.

'Gentlemen,' he said at last. 'It's been a lovely evening. We need to make an early start tomorrow.'

The ninth Inca king, Pachacuti, expanded his father's small chiefdom into a vast land empire, Tahuantinsuyu (the parts that in their fourness make a whole). The empire stretched from the Pacific coast to the jungle lowlands and south towards the pampa. Pachacuti rebuilt Cuzco, the imperial capital, in the shape of a puma (or perhaps in the shape of the empire itself). On a hillside nearby, he ordered the construction of a winter retreat where his court could enjoy the mountain scenery, hunt for deer and bathe in thermal springs.[4]

Back at the hotel, Dad and I staggered to our respective sides of the king-sized bed. After he turned out the light, I felt him shifting his weight about, trying to get comfortable. The darkened room was spinning slightly.

'Jimmy?'

'Yes, Dad.'

'Did I ever tell you about my old man?'

'Every time you have more than three beers.'

'*He* liked a beer, old John.'

'I know, you've told me.'

'Once, when he was in the navy——'

'You've told me, Dad. They dared him to jump into the dock water from the top of the mast.'

'He did it, too, the old pisshead.'

In the silence that followed, I could sense his thoughts turning to his days as a scholarship boy at a Melbourne private school.

'They used to give me shit about his old Holden at Carey Grammar.'

'I know, Dad.'

'And then they fired him from Johnson and Johnson for turning up pissed, and he bought the newsagent. Used to leave me to do Saturday stocktake and knock off down the pub...' He trailed off. For a minute, I thought he'd fallen asleep. I even started to drift off myself.

'Hey, Jimmy...'

'Yes, Dad.'

'You don't really mind doing a package tour with your old man, do you?'

'Of course not.'

'Hey, Jimmy...'

'Yes, Dad.'

'You know I'm proud of you, don't you?'

'Go to sleep, mate, it's late.'

Machu Picchu means 'old peak', in Quechua.[5] The ruined city, snuggled in a saddle between two towering peaks, is named for the mountain on which it stands. But the site may have had another name when it was a royal retreat for Pachacuti and his successor, Topa Inca Yupanqui, from the mid-fifteenth to the late sixteenth centuries. To the north, across the chasm, Machu Picchu's sister mountain, Huayna Picchu (young peak), rears like a great, grey incisor over the rest of the cordillera. Between the two, the old Inca road follows the course of the Urubamba River along the floor of the sacred valley.

'I must be like that imperturbable and crystalline river,' wrote the Peruvian novelist José María Arguedas, about a decade before he took his own life.[6]

We set out for Machu Picchu before dawn on 28 July, which happened to be Peruvian Independence Day. In Cuzco, red and white flags flew from every building – someone told us you could be fined if you didn't make the mandatory patriotic gesture. Black stone walls gleamed beneath the headlights of the minibus as it lurched through cobbled streets. I remembered the child protagonist of Arguedas's novel *Deep Rivers*, awed by the old Inca walls of Cuzco, asking his father, 'Do the stones sing at night?'

113

And his father replying, 'It's possible.'[7]

But if the stones were singing that morning, Dad and I couldn't hear them over the engine.

'We're going to Machu Picchu,' he said, flashing his teeth at me in the dark.

Later, onboard the *Macchu Picchu Express*, a man with ginger curls and pale blue eyes leaned across the aisle and touched Dad's sleeve as the train lurched and shunted away from the platform. He was older, well into his seventies, and was breathing heavily, his face a ghastly pallor.

'Tim,' he said, his voice hoarse, his accent unmistakably Australian.

'Kim,' corrected Dad.

'Sorry I missed your talk. How're you handling the altitude?'

'Not too bad for an old fart, Tony. This is my son, James. James, this is Tony Kidman.'

We nodded at each other across the cabin. I recognised from his red hair and slightly upturned nose that he was the actress Nicole Kidman's father. Tony was a well-known Sydney psychologist, a fellow veteran of the international conference circuit. He and Dad traded reminiscences most of the way to the little town of Aguas Calientes, where we caught a connecting bus to the summit.

'God, Tony's looking old,' he said, after they'd parted ways. 'Do I look that old?'

When I went for counselling during my first year as an undergraduate arts student, the therapist immediately recognised my surname in his notes.

'Halford...' said the craggy old fellow, squinting at his clipboard and casting his mind back across the years.

Brisbane psychology circles were small enough that most local practitioners knew each other.

'Oh, you must be Kim and Barb's boy. How are they?'

He'd been a colleague of both my parents. Since they'd been pressuring me for months to make the appointment, the connection was not appreciated. I didn't want them to know I'd relented.

'Well, you're from a good home. Your grades look fine. What's the problem: girls? boys?'

One of my earliest girlfriends and I had recently parted ways. In the aftermath, she'd told her large, gossipy group of female friends more detail than I would have liked about our two years of confused sexual apprenticeship. I was hiding from my social circle, reading more Dostoevsky than was good for me.

'No, nothing like that,' I told him. 'I'm thinking of changing majors from literature to psychology.'

I never arranged a second session; I booked a plane ticket instead. I spent a large part of the next decade avoiding Brisbane and my father's name.

Years later, when I was briefly home, the ex-girlfriend invited me for coffee at Wordsmiths Cafe on campus.

'I saw a doctor a few months ago,' she said.

'You're not pregnant to what's-his-name, are you?'

'No, I'm on the pill.'

'You hate the pill.'

'I know. But I went to see a specialist. Because I was experiencing some pain.'

'Ah.'

'Like I used to.'

'I see.'

115

'The doctor said I have a latex allergy. Quite a severe one.'

'Okay.'

'I thought I should tell you. Because…I wanted you to know there's nothing wrong with you.'

'That's good.'

'Or with me.'

'With you?'

'We're very happy now.'

'Ah, good.'

The North American archaeologist Hiram Bingham III made his name in 1911, when he stumbled across Machu Picchu looking for Vitcos, the last Inca capital. After being defeated by the Spanish, the Inca had retreated to a secluded location in the tropical lowlands of Peru, where they held out against the invaders for more than 30 years. When Vitcos was defeated and overrun in 1572, its location was lost. Bingham's expedition set out to find what remained.

Less than a week in, his party made a detour. At a place called Mandorpampa, an innkeeper and plantation owner, Melchor Arteaga, who Bingham referred to as 'an Indian rather better than the average, but overfond of fire-water',[8] promised to take them to see nearby ruins for a fee of 50 cents. The American wrote:

> Presently we found ourselves in the midst of a tropical forest, beneath the shade of whose trees we could make out a maze of ancient walls, the ruins of buildings made of blocks of granite, some of which were beautifully fitted together in the most refined style of Inca architecture.[9]

Arteaga has become something of a folk hero in revision-ist accounts of the discovery of Machu Picchu. Today's tour guides are at pains to point out that Bingham's 'lost city of the Inca' was not lost to the innkeeper or to other locals who lived in the area. Legend has it Bingham accepted a free lunch of sweet potatoes from farmers who were living in the ruins. They had cleared some of the overgrown Inca terraces for their crops.

The explorer, then, didn't discover this 'lost city', he merely brought Machu Picchu before the Western gaze for the first time. It was as unknown to the early twentieth-century white elites in Cuzco and Lima as it was to the conquistadors. Part of Machu Picchu's importance, as Bingham noted, was that it was 'untouched by Spanish hands'.[10] In 1912, he returned with a larger expedition to lay his own hands all over it.

My father was named Kim for the hero of Rudyard Kipling's novel. His olive complexion – so unlike my grandmother's paleness – matched her mental image of the book's protagonist, an Irish boy 'burned black as any native',[11] whose ability to pass as Indian makes him an effective spy for the British. My grandfather preferred Bill. But in this, as in many other things, he and my father were at odds. William still appears on official documents, but Dad was Kim to his mother, and Kim to his friends, and has always been Kim to us.

The two men clashed again, years later, over Dad cutting classes to attend anti-Vietnam rallies as a schoolboy. His number was never called, but he left the family home young, and for years had little to do with his father – a former navy man who believed it was young men's duty to serve. It was only with the arrival of grandsons they were reconciled.

My main memory of John Halford is of a stick-thin man who wore a too-large dressing-gown and breathed through a mask.

'Too many fags during the war,' Dad said.

I have never smoked a cigarette.

In Latin America, as in Australia, debates regularly erupt over the politics of colonial place names. Authorities have struggled to settle on the correct spelling of Cuzco, the Spanish city on the site of the old Inca capital through which all travellers pass on their way to Machu Picchu. 'Cuzco' with a 'z' is the traditional Spanish spelling of the name. It has appeared consistently in documents since the Conquest. In recent decades, however, both local and national governments have opted for 'Cusco', rejecting the letter 'z' as Spanish. A third spelling, 'Qosco', was adopted by the provincial council in the early 1990s. This version had the double benefit of differentiating the Quechua pronunciation from its hispanised gloss *and* defying the conventions of Spanish orthography (as in English, the letter 'u' must always follow the letter 'q'). Within a few years, however, 'Qosco' was dropped at the bidding of the tourism industry, which claimed the new spelling was confusing international visitors and perhaps contributing to declining revenue.[12]

Hiram Bingham begins *Inca Land* (1922) with an epigram from Kipling's 'The Explorer', a poetic manifesto and motivational pamphlet for adventurous young men of empire: 'Something hidden. Go and find it. Go and look behind the Ranges – Something lost behind the ranges. Lost and waiting for you. Go!'[13]

This swashbuckling notion of exploration was already anachronistic in Bingham's time. While his writing often channelled the nineteenth-century colonial romances of Kipling, Conan Doyle and Rider Haggard, his expeditions were state-of-the-art affairs funded and equipped by large American corporations like Kodak and Winchester, underwritten by Yale's institutional clout, and promoted energetically through the media. Bingham was a modern, self-fashioning media celebrity. It's often said he was the basis for Harrison Ford's character in *Indiana Jones*.

As an archaeologist, Bingham made a great photographer. With no formal qualifications in his academic field, he left most of the digging to others, freely roaming the site and snapping spectacular black-and-white images with a brand-new Kodak 3A special camera he'd personally cadged, free of charge, from George Eastman of Eastman Kodak. Nearly all of Bingham's theories about the origins and significance of Machu Picchu have proved incorrect. But he intuitively grasped its photogenic qualities. His photos, published in a 1913 special issue of *National Geographic*, fired the imagination of a mass audience who would one day visit the site themselves. 'The Incas,' he wrote in his accompanying feature article, 'were, undeniably, lovers of beautiful scenery.'[14]

For as long as outsiders have known about Machu Picchu, the old Inca capital of Cuzco has served as its gateway. The construction of a railway link with Buenos Aires in 1908 was already beginning to produce economic and cultural opening at the time of the first Yale expedition. After Bingham publicised his 'discovery' in *National Geographic*, Spanish guidebooks to the city and its surroundings started to appear. The flow of tourists, according to the anthropologists Pierre L. van den Berghe and Jorge Flores Ochoa, remained at fewer than twenty a day well into the 1950s.[15] 'We ascended on horseback,' wrote the Chilean poet Pablo Neruda of his 1948 visit to Machu Picchu. 'In those days there was no highway...I felt infinitely small at the centre of that navel of stone; navel of a proud and eminent, uninhabited world to which I belonged somehow...I felt Chilean, Peruvian, American.'[16]

Four years later, a young Argentine medical student, Ernesto Guevara, expressed similar sentiments in his diary – Pan-American pride and a sincere if dubious identification with Latin American indigenous cultures (his own origins were Basque and Irish): 'We found ourselves before a pure expression of the most powerful American civilisation, untouched by contact with the conquering civilisation.'[17] Like so many travellers to come, he was eager to differentiate himself from mere tourists (especially North Americans), who were already beginning to appear on the scene. 'The degenerate tribes that can be found making the journey',[18] Guevara called them. Only South Americans, with their 'semi-indigenous spirit', the young revolutionary claimed, could fully appreciate Machu Picchu. In a brilliant essay called 'Semiotics of Tourism', Jonathan Culler gives a good description of what the middle-class, non-indigenous Guevara is up to here: 'Ferocious denigration of tourists is in part an attempt to convince oneself that one is not a tourist... Part of what is involved in being a tourist is disliking tourists (both other tourists and the fact that one is oneself a tourist).'[19]

As visitor numbers at Machu Picchu increased through the 1930s and 1940s, Peruvian intellectuals of the '1909 generation' were rediscovering their country's indigenous roots. The *indigenismo* of important Cuzco figures like Luis E. Valcárcel and José Uriel Garcia sparked an Incan revival movement. Since then Cuzco has been regarded as the fountainhead of modern Peruvian identity. It has become common practice to reinvent Inca rituals, often based on the sixteenth- and seventeenth-century accounts of the 'Incan historian' Garcilaso de la Vega, and perform them at archaeological sites. The tourist industry has incorporated and marketed these rites.

During the 1960s, more affordable plane travel swelled the ranks of Guevara's 'degenerate tribe'. In 1954, just under 7000 tourists visited Cuzco, of whom only 400-odd were foreigners. By 1971, there were 40,000 foreign visitors alone.[20] After the suppression of the Shining Path guerilla insurgency in 1992, tourist numbers soared to unprecedented heights, topping 1 million for the first time in 2012.[21]

Finally, after all the queuing and the checking of tickets, all of the plane-to-train-to-bus transfers, Dad and I were inside that famous landscape, and it was, inevitably, anticlimactic. No cosmic silence descended. No Andean wisdom welled up inside us. Machu Picchu didn't seem as real laid out at my feet as it had in brochures, postcards, guidebooks and documentaries. All those steps, all those stones baking in the hard mountain sunlight gave the impression of wandering onto an abandoned film set. The way the walls seemed to move when you stared at them – an optical illusion caused by bricks of irregular sizes – contributed to the sense of unreality.

Our guide, Javier, wore a cowboy hat and waved a rainbow-coloured flag over his head. 'This way!' he cried, at the head of our tour group: 18 middle-aged Scandinavian psychologists, my father and me. Tourists often mistake the flag of the Incan Empire for the flag of the international gay pride movement. The truth is it's little older, an invention of twentieth-century Peruvian nationalists. 'This way!' Javier cried, and led us, first to the terraced agricultural zone where llamas grazed, impossibly white, against the lush grass, then to the small stone cottages of the workers' quarters, and finally to the Inti Watana stone, which points directly to the sun during the winter solstice. The Inca, Javier said, believed the stone held the sun in place. He spoke a peculiar, halting English, pausing often to adjust the position of the coca leaves stuffed into his cheeks, or to whip out a folder of laminated images that showed how certain sections of hillside or valley had been sculpted to resemble symbolic animals. Steena and Ingrid, and all the other Scandinavian therapists – hard-nosed advocates of evidence-based research in their professional lives – kept exclaiming: 'Ah, yes! I can see it now. I can see the condor.'

'Looks like a pile of old rocks to me,' whispered Dad.

The old peak flooded with people as the morning wore on, the crowds overflowing the stone vaults and houses. And what bothered us was that we were undeniably part of the flood, not observers of it. Javier would dart around a corner, then scurry back, saying, 'Too many people. This way. *Vamos!*' Other guides could be heard explaining the same features in the same words as we rushed past, sometimes cracking the same lame jokes. Javier talked on and on. He told us the Inca had expertly quarried stone for 200 buildings from the surrounding hills. He told us works teams had shaped the stone and transported it using inclined planes. He told us they had built the city walls without mortar upon a terraced mountainside to better resist earthquakes and mudslides. He had uttered these words so many times they were as dead as stones – to him and to us.

We were enormously relieved when, after three hours, he finally let us explore on our own.

When you stand at the sun gate looking down on Machu Picchu, what you are really seeing is the West's collective hallucination of how an ancient civilisation should look. The search for the 'lost city of the Inca', remember, began after the discovery of Troy and Knossos in Europe in the late nineteenth century.[22] The Argentine writer Jorge Luis Borges, who visited Machu Picchu in the 1970s when he was already blind, saw the place as clearly as anyone. In an essay on Coleridge, Borges writes about the archetype of the ruined palace in the Western imaginary. Reflecting on the strange coincidence that both Kubla Khan's 'stately pleasure dome' and Coleridge's poetic evocation of it came to them in dreams, Borges concludes the palace must be 'an eternal object' that will be dreamed and re-dreamed across human history.[23]

In 1990, Peruvian President Alberto Fujimori authorised the construction of a cable car from the valley floor to the top of Machu Picchu. Improving comfort and ease of access, he argued, would boost tourist numbers and increase revenue at a time when the country was rocked by terrorist insurgency, hyperinflation and out-of-control government debt. Opponents claimed the development would damage the integrity of the site and boost tourist numbers to well over UNESCO's recommended maximum of 2200 visitors per day.[24] The decade-long conflict that ensued illustrates the tension between regional, national and international claims to the site.

At a time when many Peruvians were hungry, people still cared enough about the cable car issue to take action. Throughout the 1990s, general strikes regularly paralysed Cuzco, and protests by students and faculty members at the city's two main universities attracted the attention of the local and international press. Hundreds of students began an annual tradition of walking from Cuzco to Machu Picchu in protest, completing in eight hours a journey most tourist hikers of the Inca Trail spread across three days, by marching along the train tracks. Peruvians abroad used their influence to lead a massive international letter-writing campaign to their government.

In 2000, as ongoing revelations of corruption and human-rights violations hounded his regime, Fujimori backed down, suspending the development indefinitely to carry out further environmental impact studies.

Late in the day, back in Aguas Calientes, we stumbled upon Tony Kidman sitting alone at the bottom of a staircase in the oncoming dusk. He gazed into nothingness, gasping for air, his face badly sunburnt.

'Are you all right, Tony?' Dad asked.

He seemed not to hear, and for a moment looked through us. Then he snapped to attention. 'Ah, Tim. It's you.' He winced. 'The altitude's still knocking me around.'

'That's no good,' said Dad. 'What did you think of Machu Picchu?'

'Hardly saw a thing.'

'Too many stairs, mate?'

'Too many years,' he replied. 'Far too many.'

In September the following year, we were saddened but not surprised to read in the papers that he'd died of a heart attack. He was only 15 years older than Dad.

Alejandro Toledo, Peru's first democratically elected President of indigenous ancestry, was sworn in at the old Inca citadel before an audience of cabinet ministers and foreign presidents on 29 July 2001, the cameras feasting on the famous scenery. He had drawn upon his background throughout the campaign, kissing Incan amulets, donning avocado necklaces and having his supporters chant the name of 'Pachacuti'. Toledo's appealing story – from shoe-shine boy to Stanford-educated economist to presidential candidate – masked his support for the same orthodox, pro-market policies as his predecessor.

Soon after his election, Peruvian negotiators led by the country's French-born anthropologist First Lady, Eliane Karp-Toledo, began pressing Yale University for the return of a large collection of artefacts – including bones, ceramic pots and Incan tools – taken from Machu Picchu by Hiram Bingham's 1912–1916 expeditions.[25] Having let the collection languish in boxes for decades, Yale scholars had commenced a new wave of research that was revolutionising understanding of the site. They were also in the process of putting together a major new exhibition of the materials.[26] The approaching centenary of Bingham's first visit to Machu Picchu in 1911 added symbolic weight to the negotiations.

125

The dispute rested on the interpretation of two decrees, one from 1912, the other from 1916, authorising Bingham to remove the artefacts from Peruvian territory. Yale argued they'd fulfilled the terms of both decrees by returning some, but not all, of the artefacts in the 1920s. The Peruvians countered that there was never any question that all objects were eventually to be returned – even if no specific timeframe was given in the decrees.

When Toledo crashed out of office in 2006, the public stoush continued. His successor as President, Alan García, was a representative of the old Lima elite who had never been overly interested in indigenous issues. But by this stage, even he could see the benefit of taking up the anti-imperialist war cry: 'Either we come to an understanding regarding...Machu Picchu, or we'll simply have to describe them as looters of treasures.'[27] In 2008, his administration filed a lawsuit against Yale through the US court system.

In the end, Yale recognised the damage to their brand outweighed the value of the collection. In November 2010, they agreed to return all but a few of the pieces. As with the handback of Uluru to traditional owners in Australia, this compromise involved co-management of indigenous cultural assets that maintained their accessibility to a broader public. Yale and the Peruvian government jointly announced that admission fees from an international travelling exhibition would be used to build a new museum and research centre in Cuzco, where the North American university would assist in an advisory role. The scandal brought this modest collection of bones and pottery – notable mainly for being dug up from the most famous of all Incan sites – to the attention of an unprecedented public audience. In Cuzco, more than 70,000 people attended the exhibition in its first year back on home soil.[28]

After seeing Tony off at the station, Dad and I decided to kill the last couple of hours before our train back to Cuzco in the thermal baths that give the town its name. Aguas Calientes was almost wholly colonised by tourism. Souvenir stores and restaurants lined both sides of the polluted stream running down the main street. At the top of the hill were the baths. Having rented towels and board shorts from a little shop out front, we changed and picked our way to the poolside. There, four fetid brown pools of bubbling water were crammed full of raucous Peruvian families, with barely a foreigner to be seen. Salsa blared over the sound system. Kids were doing dive-bombs and backflips into the deepest pool while the adults drank Cusqueña.

'Careful, gringos,' said one woman, as Dad and I slid into the water beside her. 'My sister has been farting.'

The sister shrieked and splashed her.

'That's all right, Dad and I have been holding it all day. Now we can relax.'

The women laughed, surprised we could communicate with them. They slid over to accommodate us. Both sisters were in their late forties. Their children were thrashing about, wrestling in the shadows, but neither husband was anywhere to be seen. They were drinking beer in the tub, with several empty bottles already balanced precariously on the edge.

'¿De dónde vienes?' asked the first, the cheeky one.

'Australia. Ustedes?'

'From Cuzco.'

'And you came to see Machu Picchu?'

'Yes, so the foreigners didn't have it all to themselves on Independence Day.'

Her sister giggled.

'You came all the way from the country of the kangaroos to see Machu Picchu?'

Dad interrupted to ask for a translation.

'They want to know why we came to Peru.' I told them my *papá* was a psychologist. 'He came for a big conference in Lima. I'm his translator.'

'A psychologist,' said the woman. 'Then you must help me with my oldest son.'

'After a free counselling session, is she?' said Dad. 'Which kid is hers?'

'He's in Cuzco. He doesn't like to go anywhere with his mother anymore. He's sixteen.'

When she began to speak about her son, her whole demeanour changed: 'His marks have dropped off at school. He has fallen in with a bad crowd. He misses classes and stays out late at night. I'm afraid he's drinking or taking drugs. I'm afraid he'll get his girlfriend pregnant. He won't tell me where he's been or with whom. When I try to talk to him, he shoves his headphones in his ears and turns up the volume. I'm afraid he will send himself deaf. It's my fault he is suffering. It's my fault he doesn't know his father. How can I demand discipline from him when I was undisciplined at his age?'

This took some time to translate.

'You who are an expert,' she cried, as if she could make Dad understand through the vehemence in her voice, 'what can I do to bring my boy into line?'

'Tell her I'm not an expert on Peru,' he said. 'I don't know what it is like to raise a child as a single mother in this country. All the literature says parenting varies a lot from culture to culture. If I was her therapist, I'd be able to meet with her son and hear his view. Without meeting him, it's very difficult for me to give her advice.'

The woman listened patiently through the Spanish version of all this, nodding along.

'But he must be a big expert,' she replied. 'He was invited to come a long way to talk. He must have something he can tell me.'

'All I can do,' said Dad, 'is speak to her as a parent. I've been very lucky to have raised two fine boys. In my view, the only thing you can do if your son is lost is make sure he knows you love him. Let him live his own life. Let him make his own mistakes. If he knows you love him, he will always come back to you.'

I have a photo of us together at Machu Picchu, laughing in the sunlight. We are playing roughly, like brothers, tickling each other as a stranger takes the shot. Heads thrown back, bodies blocking the famous view: there we are on the old peak, with the young peak behind.

Uluru: How to Travel
Without Seeing

While my library contains the works of travel writers, I have mostly searched for those who speak about their own place in the world.[1]

– Alexis Wright

I've spent my life gazing east. The Americas have obsessed me since my teens: rock-and-roll and the Beat writers, Latin American fiction and poetry. An east coast Australian, and a city boy through and through, it never occurred to me to see my country's desert heart until my wife R was invited to Alice Springs in September 2014, the only Mexican to give a paper at the Ecological Society of Australia's annual conference that year.

Flying home to the coast, I felt less confident in my use of the possessive pronoun. That smouldering, red-black plain didn't feel like *my country*. The terrain was as dry and rough as a scab, with the same scorched palette of colours as the dot paintings I'd seen at the Araluen Arts Centre. I could see spirals and swirls hovering over the cracked red earth. Beside me, R was watching *Charlie's Country*, Rolf de Heer's harrowing film about Indigenous Australians' experience of the Northern Territory Intervention. In 2007, the Intervention, an emergency response to allegations of alcoholism and child sexual abuse in remote communities, suspended the Racial Discrimination Act in order to apply blanket-coverage welfare and alcohol restrictions on Indigenous people in certain parts of the country, regardless of their behaviour as individuals.

Tears rolled down R's cheeks. 'Worse than Mexico,' she said, dabbing her nose with a tissue. While in Alice Springs we'd visited Monty's bar, a drinking hole fortified like a prison, where the security guard outside had looked her up and down as we approached, taking in her lovely golden skin, before deciding she was white enough, and swinging the gate open.

And then there was the Rock itself, that great, silent, ominous thing, crisscrossed by the gaze of footsore thousands. How could an outsider feel any connection to it? Less than a year earlier, I'd spent a fortnight in Peru with my father, playing the old Latin America hand. The truth was I felt less of a foreigner there.

Two boys built Uluru, playing in the mud after rain. Then, they travelled south to Wiputa, where they speared a wallaroo and cooked it. The wallaroo's tail broke in the heat of the fire, so the boys threw it away. Today, a long crack can be seen in the hillside where the tail fell. Heading north, one of the boys threw his club at a hare wallaby but missed. A fresh water spring opened where his weapon struck the ground. When the first boy refused to tell where he'd found water, his companion nearly died of thirst. Finally, the boys fought to the death. Their bodies are preserved as boulders on the top of Attila, the flat-topped mountain whitefellas call Mount Conner.[2]

Uluru's importance as a landmark has a practical dimension: it's a sandstone monolith in the desert, marking a well-watered location. But for the Anangu, its significance derives from its position within a nexus of connected places: to the east the table mountain, Attila; to the north-west, Kata Tjuta's unearthly red domes (the Olgas); and around the Rock, many smaller sites – Mutitjulu waterhole, Kantju Gorge, the caves at Kuniya Piti. Uluru stands at the crossroads of a network of Dreaming tracks the Anangu believe were once followed by ancestral beings.

The name, as far as we know, is just a toponym. It may or may not have some relation to the Yankunytjatjara for 'crying' and 'shadows'; it definitely doesn't mean 'island mountain', as literal-minded white guides have told some visitors.[3] We are a credulous bunch, those of us who approach the Rock longing for something deeper and older than the secular modernity of Australia's coastal cities – hungry for significance, ready to believe. But if Uluru has a meaning, the Anangu aren't telling.

Alice Springs is the gateway to the Rock. The 1872 inauguration of a Bush Telegraph Station in Alice – connecting Adelaide to Darwin and Australia to the rest of the world – saw more outsiders begin to arrive in the region. In its wake came labourers and bullock drivers, Afghan camel men, prospectors for gold and rubies, dingo-scalp hunters, scientists, government officials and anthropologists. The railway line, first to Oodnadatta, and later, in 1929, to Alice, also opened the interior to pastoralists. In the period from 1871 to 1891, which historian Dick Kimber calls 'the bad old days', 500 to 1000 Indigenous people were shot.[4] Even as smallpox, measles, influenza and venereal disease badly impacted the Indigenous population, European incursion pushed them from their country into reserves and missions. Settlers' overstocking of dry country, carelessness with fire, and widespread clearing of vegetation helped turn already arid land into desert.[5] Broader ecological changes, including a catastrophic drop in the central Australian mammal population, undermined the traditional subsistence economy.

A new industry was about to rise in the Red Centre.

In 1948, a truck driver named Len Tuitt graded a dirt track from Alice to the Rock and began bringing tourists in his own vehicle. He sank a bore into one side of the monolith to supply guests with water. Another important early visitor from the world beyond was Bill Harney, who in the 1950s became the first Government Ranger for the newly created Ayers Rock National Park. Harney's 1963 guidebook, *To Ayers Rock and Beyond*, marked the advent of the era of mass tourism to the site. The rise of affordable air travel also contributed. In 1961, 4000 tourists visited the Rock.[6] Nowadays, the annual total is in the order of 300,000.[7]

R's post-conference dinner was held at the Alice Springs Desert Park. Bright young postgraduates and postdocs from all over the world pumped the hands of professors, slamming down beer and exchanging business cards in the twilight. When the meet and greet was finished, we sat at a circular dining table under an open sky, the white tablecloth trailing in the sand. Food was slow to come out of the kitchen, so the after-dinner speaker, Professor Tom Griffiths from the Australian National University, was sent out early to distract the hungry crowd.

'Now I know you're all famished and you've been lectured at for the last three days,' he said. 'So I'll try to keep this to less than an hour.'

A few groans went up, but nobody complained once he started. Griffiths is an environmental historian. Australia's ecological history, he argued that night, as he does in several of his books, could help us get past the intractable postcolonial argument of settlement versus invasion. Longer environmental perspectives could diminish both apologist and apocalyptic understandings of European colonisation in 1788. That year's events were part of a series of environmental encounters and transformations. Australia's unique environment – the poorest soils in the world, a scarcity of water unparalleled on any other continent, plants that require fire to thrive, and high biodiversity – needed to be brought to the foreground of our historical narratives, he argued.[8] One perspective on Australia's contact history was to see it as an effort to understand and to cope with this particular landscape. Eventually, he said, the oldest continuous culture on earth and the first modern people to industrialise would have to work together.

Like Hiram Bingham in Peru, the 30-year-old British-born explorer William Gosse came upon the landmark for which he's remembered on his way elsewhere. His party of 'four white men, three Afghans, and a black boy' set out from Alice Springs on 21 April 1873, hoping to find an overland stock route to Perth.[9] He had sighted the Rock from a distance on an earlier expedition, but the salt marshes of Lake Amadeus prevented him reaching it. Finding and naming 'this wonderful feature'[10] was the one consolation in an otherwise unsuccessful seven-month slog.

Gosse comes across in his journals as a sober, diligent character. He gives detailed descriptions of the country through which he passes – with coordinates – for the benefit of the Surveyor General of South Australia and the Crown Lands Office. Still, beneath the unemotional tone, it is easy to detect his disappointment in the land. His report is full of gloomy descriptions: 'nothing fit for occupation', 'good country very limited, not more than thirty square miles', 'spinifex and sandhills, and dense mulga flats, destitute of water'.[11] Whereas many explorers' diaries of this period subsume the actions of the travelling party into an all-conquering narrator's 'I', Gosse is attentive to the suffering of his travelling companions, their camels and their horses: 'I think it must be in a great measure owing to the sand and spinifex that they are so distressed...their legs are raw and fly-blown.'[12] He is also a curious and gentle observer of Indigenous presence in the region: 'Two natives came for water, and after our making signs they came up to us, but seemed terribly frightened. I fancy they have heard of whites before.'[13]

It is only when he comes upon the Rock that Gosse grows excited:

Saturday, July 19. Camp in Spinifex Sandhills. Barometer 28.12 in, wind south-east...When I got clear of the sandhills, and was only two miles distant, and the hill, for the first time coming fairly in view, what was my astonishment to find it was one immense rock rising abruptly from the plain; the holes I had noticed were caused by the water in some places forming immense caves...I have named this Ayers Rock, after Sir Henry Ayers.[14]

In the Northern Territory, inconsistent signage for Uluru still reflects conflicting community views. Ayers Rock /Uluru became the Territory's first officially dual-named natural feature in 1993. In 2002, the order of the names was officially changed to Uluru / Ayers Rock at the request of the regional tourism authority.[15] Nevertheless, outside the park, on land controlled by often less than progressive Territory governments, it's still possible to find signs for Ayers Rock, named after the eighth Premier of South Australia. Inside the park, on Anangu land, Uluru has been uniformly adopted.[16]

R and I left Alice Springs early on Saturday morning in a white Hyundai Getz that would have clearly demarcated us as city slickers were it not identical to half the other cars on the road. The conference in Alice Springs must have done wonders for Avis's bottom line that weekend. But it was eerie to be part of a procession of identical white insects crawling across the desert. Nowadays, with the Stuart and Lasseter highways sealed all the way from Alice to the Rock, any old vehicle can make the journey. Also on the road that morning were dozens of motorcyclists, who roared past in clusters of three or four at a time, beards blowing, while the engine of the Getz whined at being pushed to 130 kilometres an hour. Our trip, it turned out, coincided with the culmination of the Long Ride, a charity event that saw more than 400 motorcyclists from around the country converge on the Rock to raise money for prostate cancer. Though not quite in the continent's geographic centre, Uluru has certainly, since the 1980s, become a symbolic centre, a meeting place for everyone from ecologists to bikies. In 2000, the Olympic torch relay began there.

We arrived at the camping ground of the Yulara Resort around midday, having covered 450 kilometres before lunch. There, we were allocated a patch of red earth between the campervans and trailers to pitch our tiny two-person tent, 'tadpole', which R had bought for her fieldwork in the Mexican cloud forest.

'Good luck finding a spot away from all the bloody bikes,' growled the overworked woman at reception, handing us a label for our tent and a pair of tickets that certified we were paying customers, and therefore allowed to buy alcohol at the resort.

'Don't go giving these away to anyone who shouldn't have 'em,' she said.

She wasn't, of course, referring to the bikies.

Greater separation between tourists and the Indigenous community of Mutitjulu has been one consequence of the 1985 handback to traditional owners. Gone are the days when visitors could wander through the township, indiscriminately snapping photographs of locals. In the early 1980s, the tumbledown tourist settlement near the Rock was demolished, and all accommodation, from camping to five-star luxury, was shifted 20 kilometres north, to Yulara. It's no longer the case that Uluru is 'the one place on the map where visitors and the land's original inhabitants are almost bound to come face to face', as the Australian writer Rodney Hall observed in 1988.[17] Today, the community has more privacy. It is entirely possible that daytrippers to Uluru – especially those who fly in and out of Ayers Rock / Connellan Airport and are ferried to and from the site in tour buses – will not cross paths with an Indigenous person.

During his first visit to the Rock, Gosse made a beautiful sketch of birds wheeling around its honeycombed eastern face. The first photographs, however, were taken by William Tietkens in 1889. Baldwin Spencer's photos, taken a few years later in 1894, are clearer. These early black-and-white images offer ecologists and environmental historians crucial evidence of how the land looked prior to European incursion.

In *The Biggest Estate on Earth*, historian Bill Gammage reproduces three of the earliest photos of Uluru, alongside three contemporary photos taken from the same locations.[18] Changes to vegetation in these images of the land before and after European settlement demonstrate how it deteriorated from the 1870s onward, as millennia-old Indigenous fire regimes were disrupted, and cattle were introduced.

The country around Uluru is just one case study in Gammage's monumental project of documenting Indigenous land management in Australia prior to 1788. He visits and photographs sites around the country, comparing their present-day ecology with the earliest available drawings, plans, photographs and written descriptions. Correlating masses of historical, anthropological and ecological evidence, he makes a compelling case that Indigenous people once managed the whole of Australia as a vast continental estate. There was no wilderness in Australia, Gammage insists. Through systematic and controlled burning of plants, Indigenous people provided for adverse seasons, guarded against dangerous bushfires, and moved grazing animals predictably around the country. *The Biggest Estate on Earth*, Henry Reynolds writes, 'must be the final blow to the comforting colonial conceit that the Aborigines made no use of their land'.[19]

R and I sat at a picnic shelter, shooing flies and eating a thrown-together lunch of tinned tuna on crackers. To avoid resort prices, we'd carted food supplies for the weekend in an ice-filled Styrofoam box in the boot of the car. The Rock was tantalisingly near, only a few hundred metres behind the scrub. But since we'd arrived in the middle of the day, further exploration would have to wait until the temperature dropped. Visitors are given ample opportunity to hear Anangu perspectives on the Rock inside the mudbrick Cultural Centre, *kutu warara pitjama*. Inside, we sat on the carpet of a darkened cinema and watched David Roberts and Don Murray's astonishing 1986 film, *Uluru: An Anangu Story*, co-produced with members of the nearby community of Mutitjulu. Here, an Indigenous 'we' addresses a plural, non-Indigenous 'you'. 'We want to tell you the story of this place…Our relationship to Uluru is very different to yours.'[20] Narrated and performed by community members, the film cuts between the land-rights struggle before handback, Anangu Dreaming stories and an Indigenous perspective on contact history. It is depressing how quickly the film moves from first contact – a single white missionary giving Aboriginal boys lollies – to diabetes, mission rations, assimilation, pastoral incursion, dispossession and frontier violence (of which we hear powerful first-person testimony from community members who lost family members).

But in many ways, the hopeful conclusion is more depressing still, given what has happened since. 'What has given me so much joy,' says one middle-aged woman, a traditional owner, 'is that now I have my grandmother's land back. I'm never going to leave this place. I'll remain here on my grandmother's land forever.'[21] Thirty years on, the jubilation of handback seems a terribly long time ago. At Uluru today, there is still only one Aboriginal-operated tour company, and Aboriginal staff represent a tiny minority at the Yulara resort complex. Meanwhile, the gap between Indigenous and non-Indigenous Australians in terms of life expectancy, health, educational outcomes, income and rates of incarceration remains vast. Poverty and dysfunction still scar many remote communities. During the celebrations of handback's thirtieth anniversary, the paternalistic Northern Territory Intervention was quietly extended. Originally established for 'a limited period until the situation is stabilised',[22] in the words of its architect Mal Brough, it will now remain in place, in modified form, until at least 2022.

R and I emerged from the cinema disoriented, blinking in the blazing afternoon. It was still too hot to walk around the base of the Rock, so we drove the circuit road with the air-conditioning blasting, stopping regularly, refilling our water bottles from the cask in the boot, taking the shorter trails as we went. Later in the day, we waited for sunset at the carpark, eating melted gummy bears and gazing across bullock grass and spinifex as the sky darkened slowly. While we waited, I read David Malouf's short story 'Mrs Porter and the Rock' aloud for her. Reading together was a tradition of ours, but she didn't like this story as much as I did. When we were discussing it afterwards, I realised much of my enjoyment relied on recognising specifically settler-Australian cultural types and tropes. Mrs Porter, a middle-class Anglo-Australian woman of the generation who came of age during the Depression, has been dragged reluctantly to the Rock by her wealthy, over-educated baby boomer son. In her stubborn refusal to even look at the landmark, I recognised the dynamic between my grandparents' and parents' generations, the kind of conversations they might have had if they'd travelled here together. Mrs Porter 'resents the suggestion, transmitted to her via Donald, that she had been missing out on something, some other – dimension. How many dimensions are there? And how many could a body actually cope with and still get the washing on the line and tea on the table?'[23]

Her attitudes are the product of an older, narrower Australia that hasn't disappeared by any means, but which you might not encounter if, like R, you arrived in the country in the late 2000s and lived in a capital city. And as for Mrs Porter's end, wandering disoriented and alone in the dunes: for that conclusion to make sense, the reader needed a sense of the settler-Australian trope of the interior as a place of madness and death. I could explain the cultural context for Malouf's story to someone from elsewhere. But when it came to the cultural context for Uluru, I was as lost as Mrs Porter.

The handback of Uluru to its traditional owners remains one of the symbolic high points for the Indigenous land-rights movement in Australia. When Ayers Rock National Park was created in 1950, Uluru was extracted from the surrounding Aboriginal reserve, and title was vested in the Director of the Australian National Parks and Wild-life Service. As Uluru was developing into a major tourist destination, Indigenous Australians' demands for recognition and land rights were also building momentum. Most famously, the 1967 referendum amended two overtly discriminatory sections of the Australian Constitution, at last recognising that Indigenous people should be counted 'in reckoning the number of people of the Commonwealth'.[24] Nevertheless, the Northern Territory government, the mining lobby and many settler Australians remained bitterly opposed to any suggestion the Rock should be returned to its traditional owners. In 1976, Uluru was specifically excluded from the Northern Territory Aboriginal Land Rights Act, meaning no native title claim could be made. The traditional owners persisted in their request for freehold title and a joint management plan of the kind that had already been successfully instituted at Kakadu National Park:

> We accept that our land is of interest to people all over Australia and from overseas and we are happy for them to visit and see our place. We agree to our land including a National Park. We cannot accept however, that someone else in Canberra can hold the papers to our land. It is not his country – it is ours.[25]

With the arrival of Bob Hawke's federal Labor government in 1983, the Commonwealth finally agreed to grant the Anangu freehold title to the land on the understanding it would be leased back to Parks Australia and managed in tandem. The official handback ceremony took place on 26 October 1985.

Hundreds of Indigenous people and sympathisers descended on the Rock that day to see Governor-General Sir Ninian Stephen hand the title deeds back to Anangu elders. The ceremony was not without discordant moments. As the Governor-General rose to speak, a plane flew overhead trailing a red banner: 'Ayers Rock for all Australians', to boos from the crowd. But the atmosphere was overwhelmingly positive. In his speech, the Governor-General struck a balance between emphasising the importance of Uluru to its traditional owners and acknowledging settler Australians' connection with it:

> Today we stand not merely in the centre of our continent, at its very heart, but beside what has become one of our national symbols...For many Aboriginal people, this place has still deeper meaning and deep spiritual significance, a significance whose roots go back to time immemorial. And now, today, the Uluru-Kata Tjuta Aboriginal land trust becomes the custodian of this heartland of Australia. The Trust, by the deed which is to be handed over today, acquires inalienable freehold title under Australian law to this place which is so special to its members. And at the same time, recognising, too, the special significance of Uluru to all Australians, and the appropriateness of it remaining as an Australian National Park, the Trust will today lease it back to the Australian National Parks and Wildlife Service as a National Park.[26]

My memories of the Rock are part of a composite picture of the whole trip, blurred by speed. R and I certainly didn't experience the sense of timelessness some visitors report. If anything, our time-sense felt foreshortened, intensified. Only in a wilfully ignorant postcolonial society that hasn't earned the prefix could a person believe it possible to learn something about 70,000 years of Aboriginal culture in four days. Shortness of time defined the whole nature of the experience. Leading up to the trip, we'd both crammed extra work into our calendars to clear space for it; during the trip we were always conscious of getting back in time for our return flight, and of the work commitments waiting for us at home; afterwards, we just wished we'd had more time. This is how much modern travel feels. And, I fear, much of modern life.

Sociological studies of tourism portray it variously as a pursuit of inauthentic pleasures, as secular pilgrimage, as a space for sexual permissiveness and as an opportunity to escape home identity.[27] Increasingly, however, it is viewed as a form of symbolic capital accrued as a status marker in post-industrial societies. I hate that this might be true of me. But it's hard to deny when I think of the hungry, restless, empty way I backpacked through my twenties. In 2009, the Argentine writer Andrés Neuman travelled through 19 Latin American republics on a book tour. His deadpan account of the trip parodies the notion of travel writing in the jet age by focusing mainly on neutral spaces like airport waiting lounges and hotel rooms. It was translated into English as 'How to Travel Without Seeing'.[28] That seems like a good description of our trip to Uluru. Wouldn't it be better for us and for future generations if we could learn to be happy at home? If we burned less jet fuel, and spent more time pottering in the garden? Probably.

And yet, what a thing to have been alive at a time when it's possible to move across the world in this way: to have hiked the Valley of the Winds on a hot clear Sunday; to have seen a real Namatjira gum tree blazing white against a molten-red cliff face; to have raced the darkness back to Alice, nearly running out of petrol trying to find our friends' party in the outskirts; to have slept side by side in borrowed swags on the patio; to have wallabies startle us awake near dawn, nibbling our toes; and to have gazed together at the teeming desert sky:

'Look, R, a shooting star!'

Finally, we were descending into Brisbane again, back from the centre to our coast-hugging lives. I had a lecture to write on a grim contemporary novel by an exiled Salvadoran living in Pittsburgh. R would return to her conservation report on Queensland's Brigalow Belt. The world was mashed together in odd combinations now: the Mexican ecologist surveying threats to biodiversity in central Queensland, the Australian academic working on Latin American literature. We held hands as the plane drifted down through a patch of turbulence and looked out at the city. R found it hard to understand, having arrived only a few years back, why everyone born in Brisbane wanted to leave.

'Nearly home,' she said.

'Yes, nearly home.'

It wasn't the same backwards, inward-looking place it had been 30 years ago when my parents moved north from Victoria. But the sand islands and the blue sparkle of Moreton Bay and the brown river winding through the city's heart remained. All these places had older names and histories I'd just begun to learn about – a task for a lifetime, for many generations, not for a week off work. Out in the west was the green expanse of the D'Aguilar Range, and nearby, in a labyrinth of sleepy subtropical streets as familiar as my reflection in the glass, I could see the roof of Mum and Dad's place. In the shimmering heat, the streets and suburbs looked newly made.

Porto Velho & Brasilia

In the jungle there was once a monkey
who wanted to be a satirical writer.[1]

– Augusto Monterroso

We chugged upriver at about 5 knots aboard the *Dois Irmaos*, a three-storey passenger ferry shaped like a giant wedding cake. From our hammocks on the middle deck, Valentina and I watched dense vegetation slide by for hours. It sometimes seemed we had dreamed our entire lives and had awoken for the first time. At remote riverside settlements, children ran from their thatched huts down to the muddy bank, waving as our boat passed. Maybe they were dreaming us, those kids, and all the outside world? In the canteen on the upper deck, we ate beef, rice, beans and salad three times a day, washed down with fruit juice at breakfast, and a cold can of Brahma at lunch and dinner. Then we'd return to our hammocks and read or listen to music. I was done with Faulkner and, at Valentina's insistence, was reading a collection of Spanish-language children's stories from the Ecuadorian Amazon to improve my language skills. The problem was we'd passed into Lusophone Brazil.

Every few hours, the boat stopped at one or another settlement to unload cargo. To break up the sameness, we'd go downstairs to watch the dock workers lug iceboxes full of river fish or stacks of crudely made wooden chairs down the gangway.

'Do you ever miss work?' I asked Valentina.

'Never. If I could find a way to stay on this boat forever I would.'

'I think I do. It's been five months.'

'But you study. You read a lot. You send your stories and articles to magazines. Isn't that enough?'

'I don't think it is. I think I need a job.'

'Your work ethic will make you miserable. You need to learn to just be.'

Back in my hammock, I fell asleep, listening to her pencil squeak on the page as she underlined verb forms in a Portuguese edition of Aristotle's *Poetics* – working away.

In the afternoon of the second day, Valentina shook me awake in my hammock.

'Passport check,' she said, pointing out a federal police officer in a black uniform, making his way down the line of gently rocking hammocks. Sleepily, I patted the waistband of my shorts, feeling for the bulge of my passport in the money belt I wore underneath.

It wasn't there.

After Caracas, I'd made half-a-dozen photocopies of my passport ID page, so I would never again be caught without it. Removing one of these paper copies from the secret stash down my pants, I tried to imitate the other passengers' nonchalance, passing it to the Brazilian policeman without getting up from my hammock. His eyes flicked doubtfully between the photo and my face.

'He-no-look-you.'

His Portuguese, warped by tropical fug, lethargy and hard living, was incomprehensible to me.

'¿Perdón?'

I was sure he'd now ask for the original.

'Ele não se parece como você,' he said, handing the paper copy back to me and moving away down the line.

'What did he say?' I asked Valentina, whose language skills, honed on Aristotle, left mine in the shade.

'He said it doesn't look like you because you've grown your beard and your hair long.'

My relief didn't last. Once the policeman was out of sight, I ripped off my money belt and checked all my cash and cards were in place. Even supposing some skilful, fleet-fingered thief had managed to shove his or her hand down my pants without waking me, surely they would have taken the bundle of reales, as well as my passport? No, I must have dropped it, it must be lying on the deck somewhere. Or I had absent-mindedly slipped it into the side pocket of my pack then forgotten where I'd put it. I checked the floor beneath my hammock on all fours. I piled mountains of unwashed clothing onto the deck in full view of the other passengers, emptied every pocket of my pack. And still it wasn't there. Valentina helped me explain the situation to one of the deckhands. No, they hadn't seen it; nothing had been handed in to them.

The worst scenario was the only possible one. I must have dropped it, without noticing, while embarking. The last time I'd seen it was at a passport check in the Manaus port office. We were late for the boat, last in line, dripping with sweat, freighted like cargo vessels with packs, hammocks, guitar, drinking water, snacks. The bus to the docks was already full, the driver was honking the horn. When the port official handed us our passports, we gathered our bundles and sprinted. It was easy to imagine, in retrospect, how the passport could have dropped from my hand, unnoticed, in the scramble.

'Ask him if we can call the port in Manaus,' I said to Valentina. 'It has to be there.'

'Yes, of course we can call,' said the deckhand, 'but not until we reach Porto Velho. It will only be another three days.'

I was sitting in the prow, strumming my little yellow guitar, as we finally meandered into port at sundown on the fifth day. In the west, a towering grey column of cumulonimbus blotted the fiery orange sky. The Brazilian passengers rose from their hammocks, stretching their limbs, and flooded the rooftop bar, where *forró* blared from the speakers at ear-splitting volume. Everyone but Valentina and I drank beer and danced. Soon, they formed a clapping circle around an especially energetic couple. A curvy Afro-Brazilian woman in tiny denim shorts clamped her legs around her partner's waist, throwing her head back, sweeping the deck with her long hair as she was spun in furious circles. While we lumbered down the gangway with our heavy packs, the first fat drops of rain fell. At the end of five days of stillness, we found ourselves running through unfamiliar, muddy streets. Arriving at the hotel just as the sky opened, we leaned, puffing in the doorway, and watched the main street turn into a fast-flowing torrent. It would all have been impossibly exciting, were it not for my missing passport. Without it, I couldn't cross the border with Valentina. Instead, I'd need to find my way to the nearest Australian embassy, 2500 kilometres away, in Brasília.

'Jimmy,' Dad joked when I told him via Skype, 'do you think you could have lost it somewhere *more* remote?'

'Come see me in Buenos Aires,' I said to Valentina at the Porto Velho bus station. 'I want to hear all about Bolivia.'

I realised, as we embraced, that it was the first time we'd intentionally touched, though we'd been sharing hotel rooms, double beds and tents for weeks. It was a stiff, sexless, Northern hug. We were not Latin Americans and never would be.

'Take care of yourself,' she said. 'Watch out for cops. They can tell you're nervous by looking at you. You should take up meditation.'

'I'm going to have plenty of time for it.'

The bus trip via Cuiabá took 50 hours. I spent them shivering in the freezing air-conditioning, reading to block out a noisy Chuck Norris triple feature on the TV, trying not to dwell on the passport situation. Outside, tree trunks flashed by with hypnotic monotony. Somewhere in an expanse of hours that seemed like days, we came upon a clearing as large as a city, an amphitheatre of scarred red gravel and clay beneath the sky's blue dome. At its edges, bulldozers pushed deeper into the shrinking lungs of the earth.

I arrived in the Brazilian capital on May Day, as I began my fifth month without a job. At the Pousada Nilza in the southern quarter, I took an overpriced room little larger than a cupboard. A planned city like Canberra, Brasília was built from scratch between 1956 and 1960, on a sun-scorched plateau in the country's central west. From above, it is laid out in the shape of an aircraft's fuselage, as if to reassure public servants arriving from Rio de Janeiro and São Paulo they are allowed to fly home again as soon as their work is done. This fly-in, fly-out bureacrat's paradise was designed with the motor vehicle and the aeroplane in mind. Each day, I would smear myself with sunscreen and walk prodigious distances along the baking footpaths, sweating under the brim of my Ecuadorian peasant's felt sombrero. Often, I was the only human figure in that landscape of cement, tar and glass. It was possible, in the face of Brazilian architect Oscar Niemeyer's otherworldly and beautiful white modernist buildings, to imagine yourself on some other, more rational planet. But I was in no state of mind to give his science-fiction city a fair chance. Like everyone else, I wanted to get my business done, and leave.

'You came all the way from Porto Velho by bus?' the Brazilian clerk at the Australian embassy said in English. 'How long did that take?'

'About two days.'

'You poor thing. And you're all on your own?'

'I am now.'

The embassy couldn't issue me a replacement passport on the spot, she said, because I was not carrying sufficient identification. With my Australian driver's licence, credit cards and two compliant photos, I could obtain a three-month emergency passport that would let me cross into Argentina. But it would have to be issued in Washington and couriered down. That could take as long as ten days.

'What about a visa?' I asked the clerk. 'The new passport won't have one.'

'You'll have to talk to Brazilian immigration about that.'

She scribbled an address on a scrap of paper and slid it under the plastic screen. It was for the local office of the federal police.

'Are you all right? You look pale.'

'Never been better.'

A week later, with my brand-new passport strapped securely to my body, I caught a bus to the Superintendência Regional, a treeless compound of blockish cement buildings and dead brown grass that never features in lists of Brasília's architectural marvels. All week, I'd been reading horrific stories online about the Brazilian feds storming into Rio's favelas with automatic weapons. But the local branch was different. I was escorted into a messy office where a plump, smiling man with a blond beard was watching a documentary on tortoises.

'*Animais maravilhosos,*' he said, slowly shaking his head. 'Marvellous animals. Take a seat. The embassy called me about you. How do you pronounce your name?'

'James.'

'H-a-mesh. Good. I'm José. Let's get this sorted.'

To finalise the matter, José needed me to give him a step-by-step account of the circumstances in which I had come to be '*clandestino*' in Brazilian territory. I would have to give him enough detail to file a two-page written report on the matter to his superiors. Unfortunately, his English was as basic as my Portuguese, and his Spanish wasn't much better. We were forced to communicate painfully slowly in a mix of Portuñol and beginner's English, with much frantic gesturing. To ask me my date of birth, he hummed the tune to 'Happy Birthday'. Every few minutes, he'd get distracted from his muddled report by a fascinating fact about tortoises.

'That Australian guy, the crocodile hunter, has one called Harriet in his zoo.'

At last, he took my fingerprints, fined me 165 reales, and put the first stamp in my new passport.

'Sorry, what does that mean? What do I do about a new visa?'

'That stamp? Don't worry about that. It means you have three days to leave the country.'

'Or what?'

'Or you'll be deported.'

When all the paperwork was finalised, he shook my hand, smiling hospitably, and said in his best English, without the slightest discernible trace of irony: 'Welcome to Brazil.'

Coetzee in Buenos Aires

The heads of Antipodeans turn upwards.[1]

– Murray Bail

Late on a Monday afternoon in April 2016, I crossed Buenos Aires to hear J. M. Coetzee give a speech. The journey took two and a half hours. I left the cobbled streets, antique stores and tourist crowds of colonial San Telmo, rode the subway to Retiro Station, and caught a commuter train on the Mitre Line that took me about 25 kilometres north-west of the centre. As we departed the downtown area, broad boulevards and grand public buildings made way for factories, freeways and drab apartment blocks. I disembarked at Miguelete, the second-last station, which is located outside the city limits on the edge of the *conurbano*, the ring of industrial and working-class neighbourhoods surrounding the federal capital. Imagine a version of western Sydney with upwards of 10 million residents. Densely populated, growing fast, and vital to winning government nationally, Greater Buenos Aires is hugely important to the country economically and culturally. But because nearly 40 per cent of the population lives in poverty,[2] and because it's been the heartland of Peronism, the populist workers' movement that's dominated Argentine politics since the 1940s, the *conurbano* is often represented as a menace in the mainstream Argentine media. When I asked a group of students for directions to the university campus, they led me through a suburb of low-set cement buildings, pot-holed streets and rubble. We cut through an old railway yard where carriages lay rusting in long grass and squeezed through a gap in the chain-link fence.

The Universidad Nacional de San Martín (UNSAM), a smallish public university with 23,000 students, just celebrated its twenty-fifth anniversary. The location of the main campus brings a sense of solidarity with marginal communities and informs the university's research agenda. There's a large centre dedicated to studies of the global South. In 2014, the rector Carlos Ruta pulled off something of a promotional coup when he persuaded J. M. Coetzee to visit twice a year to direct a seminar series on 'Literatures of the South'. The event brings high-profile South African and Australian writers and critics to Argentina to work with local postgraduate students and writers. It aims to develop comparative perspectives on the literatures of the three countries, to establish new intellectual networks, and to build a corpus of translated works from across the South through collaborative publishing ventures. So far, the project has led to the publication of new Spanish translations of the Australian writers Nicholas Jose, Gail Jones and Delia Falconer, the South Africans Zoë Wicomb, Ivan Vladislavić and Antjie Krog, and the Mozambican Mia Couto – all by the Argentine press UNSAM Edita – and to the publication of English translations of novels by the Argentine writers Mariana Dimópulos and Marcelo Cohen – published in Australia by Giramondo.

After a harp and flute recital, and a ceremonious welcome from the vice-rector, Coetzee rose to speak before about a hundred people in a darkened auditorium. He was dressed in Nobel neutral: a smartly cut black jacket but no tie, his white shirt buttoned tightly at the throat. His voice was soft, his accent shorn of any local indicator – there was no Cape Town, London or Adelaide in it. He read from his notes very slowly and clearly, pausing often, weighing each syllable. I didn't notice him trip up once. About half the audience wore headphones to hear the simultaneous translation. It felt as though we had stumbled into a scene from *Elizabeth Costello*. In Coetzee's 2003 novel, a celebrated Australian writer spends the twilight of her career travelling the world, from small-town Pennsylvania to a cruise ship bound for Cape Town, lecturing on traditional humanist subjects such as 'Realism' and 'The Future of the Novel'. Costello's journeys between indistinguishable centres of global culture act as a narrative frame for her lectures, and often ironise or unsettle their arguments. As the book progresses, she becomes increasingly unsure of her principal claims about the novel: its ability to imaginatively bridge the gap between self and other, its relationship to a national readership. 'The word–mirror is broken, irreparably, it seems,' she concedes to one audience.[3]

Coetzee shaped his speech to the place where he was standing. He presented himself as a writer who had lived most of his life in two regions of the South, now visiting a third.[4] Like many contemporary academic critics, Coetzee spoke of literature as a worldwide system in which power is unevenly distributed. But the novelist focused squarely upon the consequences of this dynamic for the least powerful literatures. The politics of translation and publishing in the Southern Hemisphere was a key theme:

> By and large, Australian writers reach Australian readers via publishing houses based in Europe; I believe the same is true, mutatis mutandis, of Argentine writers and the Argentine public. For writers from the South, being published in the North before they are re-exported to the South can mean that they need to follow norms and conform to standards set in the North.[5]

South–South publishing ventures set out, on a small scale, to challenge that arrangement.

Unlike Elizabeth Costello, Coetzee stuck strictly to script. His speech discussed the problems and potential of a South–South framework for comparative literary studies. Since the end of the Cold War, he noted, North–South terminology has replaced the older frameworks of centre and periphery, or First, Second and Third worlds, in the sociological literature. All of these terms describe a pattern of inequality in power, wealth and cultural influence that grew historically out of first European and later North American imperialism. Australia, a wealthy peripheral nation of the Southern Hemisphere, in some ways unsettles the North–South binary, revealing its basis in economics not geography. Yet Australian literature, no less than those of Argentina and South Africa, has struggled to free itself from a sense of cultural dependency and inferiority, on the one hand, and from nationalist exceptionalism on the other. All three countries feel the weight of what Coetzee, in his UNSAM address, termed 'the Northern Gaze'. Drawing on the ideas of the Australian sociologist Raewyn Connell, he has used the 'Literatures of the South' seminars to call for a comparative literary studies of the South less concerned with 'writing back' to the old imperial centres than with learning to 'ignore the gaze of the North' and 'to see the South as home'.[6]

The speech concluded with the novelist's own 'heterodox' perspective on the South. It was the view, he stressed, not of a theorist, but of a practising writer:

> In my view 'South' will in due course suffer the fate of 'periphery', of 'Third World', and of other specialist terms of the social sciences...What is left is the real South, the South of this real world, where most of those present in this room were born and most of us will die. It is a unique world – there is only one South – with its unique skies and its unique heavenly constellations. In this South the winds blow in a certain way and the leaves fall in a certain way and the sun beats down in a certain way that is instantly recognisable from one part of the South to another. In the South, as in the North, there are cities, but the cities of the South all have a somewhat phantasmatic quality. The peoples of the South are all, in one way or another, rough and a bit lazy. We have troubled histories behind us, which sometimes haunt us. It is nothing like this in the North. I can go on endlessly with my list. And the literatures of the South do indeed go on endlessly as they try to pin down in words their intuitions of what a life in the South consists in.[7]

I suspect what Coetzee means by the 'real South' may come more clearly into focus when counterposed with its opposite, 'the mythic South', which he employed in an earlier speech at the UNSAM to refer to the South as it has been imagined by the North. The huge body of literature by the North about the South stretches from the near present back into antiquity: the South Sea tales of Poe, Swift, Defoe and More; European narratives of exploration and conquest; the opposition of the Boreal and Mediterranean moods in the work of Paul Celan, Gottfried Benn and Nietzsche; the cosmogonies of Augustine and Ptolemy; Boreas and Notos, the Greek Gods of the North and South winds. This mythic South, an 'imagined geography' constructed through metropolitan discourse, is beginning to be studied in the same way Edward Said examined Western mythologies of the Orient. It is the locus onto which the North projects its fantasies, the North's Other.

The real South, one presumes, is the opposite: the South seen through Southern eyes. For the time being this elusive entity can probably only be glimpsed. Coetzee's two fascinating speeches delivered in Argentina formulate the opposition of the mythic and real Souths as an imaginative stimulus, not a theory. We should know better than to expect further explanation. Just as the narrative framing of Elizabeth Costello's lessons suggests a mistrust of universalising theories, Coetzee's recent fiction, as James Ley has noted, 'displays a neo-romantic suspicion that reason is an enclosed and self-validating system'.[8] The first two 'Jesus' novels (rumour has it a third is coming) were written across the period that Coetzee was visiting Argentina regularly, and are set in an unnamed Spanish-speaking country. The country is not Argentina or any other Latin American republic 'in this real world', but it is clearly located in the South. These recent fictions – focused on the relationship between the stolidly rational Simón and his wildly imaginative adopted son David – more fully elaborate Coetzee's richly suggestive ideas about the interplay of North and South.

Afterwards, I shared a cab back to town with a couple of administrative staff from the university and a Chilean translator who told me he had worked with the writer on Spanish versions of two further lessons of Elizabeth Costello. The Belle Époque facades and neon billboards of downtown Buenos Aires came back into view: bars, steakhouses and all-night bookstores, a mural of Eva Perón overlooking a huge homeless encampment, hundreds of posters of the recently ousted Peronist President Cristina Kirchner, graffiti protesting the austerity measures imposed by her successor, Mauricio Macri, a stray dog drinking from a puddle outside a shuttered HSBC. Candles flickered beneath an underpass in the ruins of an old torture chamber. We were back in the centre: the place that is neither North nor South, but somehow both at once.

A year later, I returned to the UNSAM to present an academic paper at a conference about Coetzee. The presenters came from as far afield as the Netherlands and Austria, but most were from the region: Mexico, Colombia, Brazil, Chile and Argentina. It must have been strange for Coetzee to sit through two days of talks about his own work, delivered in a foreign language. This time, he listened to most of the presentations without simultaneous translation, suggesting his Spanish had come along in the intervening year. His presence created a frisson in the room: even the full professors were slightly overawed. One nervous young Colombian postgraduate student forgot the name of a secondary character in the novel *Disgrace*.

'You know...the African neighbour...' he stammered.

'Petrus,' chorused half the room, eager to help.

I thought I saw Coetzee laugh along with the rest of us.

We spoke briefly after my paper, which was about several Australian writers who have imitated Borges and Coetzee's habit of inventing imaginary authors.

'I have a good Borgesian story for you,' he said. 'An academic friend was in the US recently, teaching a course on Australian literature. Apparently, they all kept asking him what he knew about the novelist Elizabeth Costello.' A wry smile played across his face as he turned away to attend to an autograph seeker. 'Send my best to R,' he added.

In the evenings, after Coetzee retired to his hotel, a dozen of us went for dinner downtown. Buenos Aires worked its familiar magic on us: one minute it was half past ten, the next it was one in the morning and, though we had only shared two bottles of wine between us, we were drunk on good company and literary gossip. Naturally, everyone had a Coetzee anecdote:

'He flew all the way from Adelaide to Mexico for a symposium I organised. He's nearly eighty. It was a huge effort.'

'After he visited us in Brazil, he gave me access to his letters for a research paper I was writing. People think he's fearsome, but he's the gentlest man.'

'He agreed to be a referee for me when I was desperate for a job.'

The next day, the conference concluded with a stage adaption of Coetzee's classic 1986 novel *Foe*, in which the female castaway, Susan Barton, gives readers an alternative perspective on Robinson Crusoe and Friday's famous island. 'The true story is buried within Friday, who is mute,' she concludes. 'The true story will not be heard till by art we have found a means of giving voice to Friday.'[9] I thought that my critical faculties might have been dulled by my sentimental attachment to Argentine Spanish, but everyone agreed afterwards that the production *was* very good. Live musicians played a moody score for cello and electronic percussion; Crusoe and Friday were represented by huge shadow puppets projected onto a screen; the female lead chanted her lines like a *porteña* poetess at a salon. Coetzee, normally undemonstrative, was visibly moved. After the curtain fell and the cast returned to acknowledge the crowd, he leapt from his front row seat and stormed onstage to embrace the actors in turn. Buenos Aires had got to him, too.

Parque Lezama

And even sadness was also something for
rich people, for people who could afford it.[1]
— Clarice Lispector

Brasília to Buenos Aires, at well over 3000 kilometres, was
the longest leg of all. Having come this far by land, I was
determined not to fly. In the chilly air-conditioned interior
of the bus, I went into a kind of hibernation. Gone was
the euphoria of Roraima and Manaus. I could no longer
motivate myself to read or write or even watch a movie. I
slept without dreaming through epic stretches of highway.
Eating tasteless platefuls of roadhouse *feijoada* was a joyless
chore; so was all interaction with the driver, waiters and
other passengers. It was a relief to be back in my seat again,
indifferently surveying the changing landscape. Passing
through the bleak, industrial outskirts of São Paulo, I felt
no inclination to explore further. I was utterly incurious,
grateful not to have to negotiate that pulsing, concrete
nightmare of a city. Somewhere north of Florianópolis, my
mood lifted for a minute at the sight of the Atlantic: beach
umbrellas and volleyball nets on a sandy curve of bay, lazy

breakers on the hazy silver sea. Then we turned inland again, passing through long tracts of undulating cleared grassland, grazed by reddish-brown Brahman cattle. Further south, I recognised we were entering my home latitudes. The sight of hilly green country and palm trees reminded me of the Sunshine Coast hinterland. My body ached all over. I spent six or seven hours on a bench seat outside an evangelical church in Porto Alegre, waiting for a connecting bus. An Afro-Brazilian woman, dressed all in white, invited me inside, but I could only shrug at her. I was too exhausted to reply. If they had sung better, I might have accepted Christ, but their hymns sounded like advertising jingles, and the gringo preacher's accent in Portuguese infuriated me. The sun was setting as we drove south. I slept through Uruguay. By the time I woke, all was black outside. For an instant, the headlights shone upon the white trunks of a stand of eucalypts on the bare plain – then they were gone. I could hear the wind ripping through bullrushes and pampas grass. When we disembarked for dinner, it was only nine or ten degrees. I shivered in my one thin sweater. At first light, the bus finally skirted the muddy-brown River Plate, where cargo ships already plied the choppy surface. The sky was streaked with feathery cirrus above the cranes and skyscrapers of restless Buenos Aires.

I was awoken by two voices, an Australian man and an English woman, whispering urgently on the far side of the darkened hostel dormitory.

'I don't want to,' said the English woman. 'I just want you to hold me.'

'Come on, what did you come back here for?'

'I don't know.'

Checking my watch, I found I'd been asleep for 14 hours.

'You were all over me at the club.'

'But now I feel sick.'

'Bullshit.'

I heard bodies shifting, a creaking mattress, heavy breathing.

'I said I don't want to.'

'Come on.'

I coughed once, loudly.

'There's someone there,' she said. 'Let's just sleep. Let's just hold each other.'

'Get out of my bed, you silly bitch. I'm serious. Go back to your own hotel. I'm not gonna lie here all night with a pricktease.'

They rose and left the room, their angry voices receding down the corridor towards reception. A few minutes later, he returned alone.

'Fuckin' women,' he said. 'Where are you from?'

'*No hablo inglés.*'

Next morning, I checked out before the Australian woke up, and found a private room in a rundown pension in San Telmo. I was done with hostels. But I certainly wasn't ready to go home.

I spent June in Buenos Aires looking for a job. In the afternoons, I browsed advertisements online, revamped my CV at the Internet cafes, and made contacts through various expatriate networks. In the mornings, I took a big bag of oranges I'd bought at the Chinese grocery store on the calle Defensa to the Parque Lezama and ate breakfast. The reason my room at the pension was so cheap, it turned out, was that neither the heating nor the hot water were functioning. I had a heavy cold and a cough that I couldn't shake for weeks, but wouldn't take any medicine or see a doctor. I was punishing myself for the passport fiasco in Brazil.

Finding myself with no one to talk to in a city of prodigious and passionate speech, I bought a set of chess pieces and played against myself, rugged up against the wind, at the tables in the amphitheatre at the northern end of the park. There was a Russian Orthodox cathedral across the street, and a statue of the conquistador Pedro de Mendoza nearby. Some historians still argue that this hilltop, with its privileged outlook, is the place where the Spaniards first 'founded' the city of the fair winds, in 1536, before it was decimated by hunger and hostile tribes, only to be re-established another 40 years later.

'Hard to believe Buenos Aires had any beginning,' Jorge Luis Borges once wrote. 'I feel it to be as eternal as air and water.'[2] And it is hard to imagine this place without buildings or roads when you stand on that hilltop in the city's south and listen to the tidal roar of traffic on the Avenida Colón.

One day in the park, a woman sat beside me and stared at the side of my face. I chewed my empanada. Six months on the road had trained me to avoid eye contact with strangers. But there she was, only centimetres away. She was pale, gaunt, and wore a grey tracksuit. She seemed much older than me, though I suppose she was only in her thirties. Her hacking cough matched mine. I don't remember the colour of her eyes, but I remember the whites looked huge. She had an addict's twitchiness, but I never saw her take anything.

'Are you hungry? Here, have one.'

Three more empanadas were wrapped in newspaper on the tabletop, grease leaking through yesterday's headlines. Steam rose from the bundle when I opened it. It smelled inviting.

'Go ahead, take one. There's chicken, beef and corn.'

Cautiously, she accepted. She nibbled at the pastry for a moment, then wolfed it down in a couple of bites.

'You live around here?'

'In the shelter.'

'What's your name?'

'Corina.'

'Like the song?' I cleared my throat and croaked out the tune for her: 'Corina, Corina, where you been so long?'

'I don't know it,' she said, helping herself to a second empanada. Then a little smile. 'But it sounds like shit.'

One night in the pension's shared kitchen, I found a beautiful dark-haired girl my own age squatting before the oven, weeping.

'What's the matter?'

'I can't get it to light.'

'It's easy, let me show you.'

She passed me the matches.

I cooked her gnocchi that night and we shared my 6-peso bottle of merlot in the lounge by the lobby, the only room where the heating worked. Margarita was majoring in pure maths in Bogotá, but was taking a semester off to visit friends in Buenos Aires. Her English was good, delivered with a thick American accent because she often holidayed in Miami, where her father kept a house. He was mayor of a town I'd never heard of. Her mother had died when she was three. That was why she couldn't cook: in her household, the servants had done everything.

'This is the first time I've been away without Papá. I'm discovering that I'm basically a useless person.'

Colombia, as it happened, was playing Argentina in the soccer that night, which presented her with a dilemma.

'If I support my country, people here will want to kill me and if I support Argentina, I'll be a traitor. Let's support Australia.'

'You can't support Australia in a match between Argentina and Colombia.'

'Of course you can. Have some more wine.'

Corina and I ate breakfast together most mornings for a month. Sometimes we would have fruit with yoghurt, or bread and jam, but steaming hot empanadas from the family-run restaurant on the calle Defensa were our favourite. Corina's company and her help with my Spanish were worth their weight in empanadas. She told me she was looking for a job, too. She'd been a maid for seven years in her hometown of Rosario, up north. Her boss had fired her, three years ago, for stealing.

'It was a lie. She didn't like the way her husband looked at me.'

'What about your family?'

She looked away, spat a lump of yellowish sputum in the dirt.

When she was feeling well, we would often play chess. It only took her a week to learn the rules. Her smile, the first time she beat me, was spectacular – better than Iguazu Falls. On bad days, her mood plunged. She cursed me, coughed uncontrollably and swore she was dying of lung cancer. Once, she begged me to take her back to the pension.

'I want to be fucked one last time before I die.'

'Not in my bedroom you don't. It's as cold and dark as a tomb.'

One day, Margarita and I decided to have a late lunch in Chinatown — she'd never tried Chinese. It had to be mid-afternoon, I explained, so I could keep my daily appointment with Corina.

'Let me check I understand…You have breakfast every day with a homeless woman in the park?'

'That's right.'

'Why?'

'For the company.'

After lunch, we went on to the Japanese garden in Palermo, where she asked me to take her picture under the cherry trees. A few brave blossoms were still resisting the June cold, but the branches were mostly bare. We held hands on the curved red bridge, watching orange carp with dead eyes stare up at us from the green water.

'My boyfriend left me last month after four years.'

Beyond the tranquil boundary of the garden, street vendors were hawking newspapers, hot corn, sandwiches, raincoats.

'Aren't you going to say something?' she said.

'I guess there are worse things than loneliness.'

On the first sunny morning in weeks, I took a proper breakfast of two hot coffees and half-a-dozen *medialunas* to the park. Corina was calm again, but ate little as I told her my news.

'I think I've found a job at a public school in the provinces. Sixteen teaching hours a week. No salary, just food and board. It's perfect.'

She refused my offer of fruit and yoghurt.

'Do you want to play chess?'

'No.' She spat on the ground. 'It isn't fair.'

'What isn't?'

'I've been looking for a job for three years.'

The cruelty of my announcement hadn't even occurred to me. I'd expected her to be pleased.

Margarita sent me a text message that afternoon.

'Changed 2 hotel with heating round corner. Come visit.'

A few other young foreigners were staying there: a scruffy Frenchman who'd been on the road for five years, funding his travel by winning at poker in youth hostels; a dour Danish anthropologist studying the lesbian tango community in Buenos Aires. Margarita demonstrated her mathematical prowess by trouncing us all at cards, even the Frenchman.

'It must be time for me to go home,' he said.

At a noisy bar, we drank until I was brave enough to kiss Margarita. We spent the night in my room, but she told me she was on her period.

'Anyway, it's much too cold to make love,' she said.

We held each other for warmth without undressing.

Corina didn't reappear in the park for three days, so I ate breakfast for both of us. At our previous meeting, we'd written her résumé on the back of a crumpled napkin. Today I'd brought a dozen typed and printed copies she could distribute. But it looked like she wasn't coming. It was too cold to concentrate on studying Spanish or reading with a dictionary. The wind tore leaves from the treetops. Even under three layers of second-hand clothes, I found myself shivering. I walked a brisk circuit of the park to warm up and noticed for the first time that the statue of the Roman Capitoline Wolf was suckling only one baby. Thieves had stolen Remus.

A message arrived from Margarita.

'Have met a very special boy and will not b able to c u again. Thanx 4 being a good listener. Send me ur email.'

I erased it instantly. I erased the other dozen or so messages she'd sent me and deleted her number from my phone. My head sank onto the chessboard. Sitting in the amphitheatre, I read over Corina's résumé: an incomplete high-school diploma, seven years in one job with no reference, three years out of work, no fixed address. Printing copies of it was not going to help; nothing I could do was going to help. I felt as useless as Margarita trying to light the stove. I didn't even know how to care for myself.

Corina arrived mid-afternoon, later than she'd ever come before. But it was the Corina with bulging eyes and spit dangling from her lips.

'Take this,' she said, thrusting a scrap of paper at me. I only had a chance to glance at it before she snatched the manila folder I was holding and flung it to the ground in front of me, spilling the printed copies of her résumé. She struggled to speak between explosive bursts of coughing.

'*¡Hijo de puta!* I have cancer. I'm going to die. Why won't you fuck me before I die?'

'Corina. I'm going to go now.'

'*¡Hijo de puta!* There is a job for you, but there's no job for me.'

On the bus trip south to San Miguel del Monte, the town on the edge of the pampa where I would be teaching, I kept thinking about Corina and Margarita, the two women I'd met in Buenos Aires. I couldn't tell if I was the one who was leaving or the one who'd been left. The note Corina had given me seemed to be an extract from an Argentine self-help book. I've lost it now. I can only remember one line:

'Forget past mistakes. Keep moving forward.'

Such Loneliness in That Gold

*I have also wondered if most women…are not, by necessity,
the great and unacknowledged storytellers of this country.*[1]

– Delia Falconer

In 1976, Jorge Luis Borges dedicated a poem called
'The Moon' to María Kodama, a shy, beautiful, Japanese-
Argentine woman, 37 years younger than him:

> There is such loneliness in that gold.
> The moon of the nights is not the moon
> Whom the first Adam saw. The long centuries
> Of human vigil have filled her
> With ancient lament. Look at her. She is your mirror.[2]

Their story is well known in Argentina. They met in 1953
in a bookstore on the calle Florida in downtown Buenos
Aires.

'Excuse me. I heard you give a lecture when I was a little
girl.'

'Ah, did you? And now you're all grown up?'

'No, I'm in high school. In my fourth year.'[3]

She was 16 and he was 54 – already famous in Argentina, but not yet abroad. He was about to lose what was left of his sight. 'He only saw light and shadow. But from my voice he would have known I was very young.'[4] Borges invited Kodama to join his Saturday morning Anglo-Saxon study group at the National Library, where he was director.

'Old English? Like Shakespeare?'

'No, much older. Tenth century.'

'It must be very difficult.'

'Yes, but I don't know it either. I am proposing that we study it together.'[5]

They married in 1986, two months before he died.

I met María Kodama at the Persicco, a cafe in the upscale Buenos Aires neighbourhood of Recoleta, on a grey Sunday morning in May 2016. Outside, the Avenida Corrientes was slick from the previous night's storm, strewn with yellow and orange leaves. A homeless man playing chess at the table by the entrance was shouting at his invisible opponent. As Kodama pushed through the glass doors, looking for me, I felt a surge of nervousness. We'd arranged to meet earlier in the day but had rescheduled because of a mix-up about the location. She could be prickly, my Argentine friends had warned. 'You're meeting the FIFA of Argentine literature,' one young Buenos Aires poet said. 'Watch out she doesn't sue you.'

She was a slender woman, a little shorter than I expected. Dressed smartly but simply in a cream-coloured jacket and grey scarf, she wore a silver bangle on her right wrist, and large, square rings on the first and third fingers of her left hand. Though the Argentine press delight in printing unflattering photographs of her, Kodama never wears makeup; entering her eighties she isn't about to change. As in nearly all the pictures I'd seen, she wore light colours – a carefully considered choice, I suspect, from someone well aware the word 'widow' will appear prominently beneath every image. She smiled as I rose to greet her. When she kissed my cheek, I forgot, in my relief, to call her señora: 'María, *perdón*. I'm sorry for the confusion. I'm an academic not a journalist.'

'*No te preocupes*. It's better you're not a journalist.'

The Persicco is a noisy, modern place with white and yellow checked tiles and shiny brass fixtures. Some of the other customers stared at her, whispering among themselves, as we sat down together. Kodama gave me the best part of three hours of her time, describing her life with Borges and discussing his work. Her generosity and warmth were at odds with everything I'd ever read or heard about her.

Relatively little is known about María Kodama's early life. Her father, Yosaburo Kodama, was born in Japan in 1905, and was raised by his grandmother, his only relative. When she died, he left his homeland for good. Kodama doesn't know the exact year of his departure or his reasons for emigrating. He was one of thousands of young Japanese who left for the Americas between the 1868 Meiji Restoration and the Second World War. Better economic prospects and avoiding conscription into the imperial military were common motives. As restrictions on Asian immigration were introduced in the north, increasing numbers settled in Latin America.

Yosaburo planned to go to the USA, with a stopover in Argentina to visit a friend of a friend. But in Buenos Aires, he met and fell in love with a 17-year-old Argentine-German pianist named María Antonia Schweizer. Kodama says María saw Yosaburo as 'an exotic prince from faraway lands'. He was nine years older than her. Though he soon found work with a pharmaceutical company in Buenos Aires, the marriage was unhappy, and the couple separated when their daughter was only three years old. María Kodama won't talk about her brother, Jorge: 'Let's just say I'm an only child.'[6]

Born on 10 March 1937, Kodama grew into a shy, solitary girl, with few friends of her own age, and certainly no boyfriends. She lived with her staunchly Catholic mother and grandmother but spent weekends with her Japanese father: 'I was brought up between two cultures. My grandmother was all about God, the Fatherland, and the family home; my father was a Shintoist. One would say white and the other would say black...I had to choose or I would have gone mad.'[7]

Kodama chose Japan. Until she met Borges, Yosaburo Kodama was the most important person in her life. Kodama remembers him teaching her the basics of the Japanese language and telling her stories of the country's history and culture. He also contributed to her aesthetic education: 'My father liked art very much. From a very young age, he gave me books of paintings and took me to exhibitions.'[8] On one of their weekend excursions she asked him to define beauty. The next week, by way of an answer, he gave her an art book containing an image of a sculpture in the Louvre, the *Winged Victory of Samothrace*.

'But it doesn't have a head.'

'Who told you that beauty is about the head? Look at the folds of the tunic. They're being blown by the wind off the sea. To capture the sea breeze for eternity, that's beauty.'[9]

Kodama often says she was drawn to Borges because his ethical and aesthetic outlook reminded her of her father. 'Borges always joked that my father had educated me for him, because thanks to all that training in my younger days, I could later describe for him the reality he could no longer see.'[10] The two men met on several occasions but were not close.

Kodama has told the story of her first encounter with Borges's writing in dozens of interviews and public speeches. When she was five years old her private English tutor read her Borges's 'Two English Poems', which he dedicated to Beatriz Bibiloni Webster de Bullrich, one of many respectable Buenos Aires society ladies he unsuccessfully courted in the 1930s. She repeated this favourite anecdote to me: 'In these poems, which are in English because it was the language he spoke with that señora, he lists all the things he can offer her, and they are the opposite of what one might expect. He offers her his solitude, his sadness, his failure and 'the hunger of my heart'. When she [the tutor] translated this for me, I asked her, 'What is hunger of the heart?' because obviously for a five-year-old child, hunger is only the need to eat. She told me I would understand when I grew up.'

María Kodama has never remarried and has never had children. She has dedicated her life to promoting Borges's work through the foundation she runs in his name. I thought that by pushing her to talk a little less about him, and a little more about herself, I might steer her away from the official narrative. But I found her reluctant to emerge from his shadow.

'Can you describe an ordinary week in your life?'

'I travel a good deal to talk about Borges's work overseas. When I am at home in Buenos Aires, I spend a lot of time at home reading. Many people ask me to comment on theses or academic studies about Borges.'

'But for fun?'

'I don't have a television set or an email account. I go to a live show nearly every night: music, theatre or dance. Last night I saw the Shen Yun dance troupe from China. They are very interested in Borges in China nowadays. The complete works have been translated into Mandarin.'

Since her answers kept spiralling back to Borges, I tried another angle. I knew she had studied literature at the University of Buenos Aires and had noticed she always made a point of being introduced in public as a writer, translator and teacher, though most people know her as Borges's wife. So, I asked her what she had written and whether any of her work had been published. She laughed: 'I have never published anything because I am always writing prologues for other people's books. I write for pleasure. Borges adored the short stories I used to write and wanted me to publish them. He wanted to write the prologue, but I never let him do that.'[11]

Kodama didn't even mention her forthcoming book, which was published a few months after we spoke. *Homenaje a Borges* is a collection of 20 serious-minded lectures about Borges's work that Kodama has delivered at various universities around the world since his death. Its one unguarded moment is the dedication: 'To Borges, my love for ever and ever and a day.'[12] The only piece of creative writing I managed to find published in her name was a brief memoir that appeared in the *New York Times* in 2011, in which she described the view from her apartment. Her window looks onto Borges's old library, a building full of 'books once touched by his hands'.[13]

By the late 1960s, the bond between Borges and Kodama had evolved beyond friendship. The biographies are unanimous that it lacked any physical dimension; I was too polite to ask. Aside from their regular language studies, they took to meeting at the patisserie La Fragata, and at his home, where she would assist him with translations, transcribe new work and read aloud for him from his favourite books. In those years, Kodama studied literature at the University of Buenos Aires, where Borges was a professor, and she earned a living teaching Spanish to Japanese businessmen. She had worked hard to establish financial independence from her family, who disapproved of the professor's frequent telephone calls and gifts of books. It was Borges, blind and unmarried in his sixties, who continued to live with his mother. Under the watchful eye of Leonor Acevedo de Borges, the professor and his protégé exercised an almost Victorian level of propriety in the decade of free love. Kodama dressed modestly in white blouses and plaid skirts, and the two always addressed each other with the formal '*usted*' in place of the familiar '*tu*'.

'She liked me, and we respected each other,' Kodama says of Doña Leonor.[14] For most of Borges's adult life, the writer's mother acted as his carer, literary secretary and travelling companion. As Doña Leonor's health declined and her son's fame increased, the bachelor sought a wife. Between 1967 and 1970, during Borges's short-lived, unhappy first marriage to Elsa Astete Millán – a widow, and an old flame from the 1940s – Kodama was apparently the only woman allowed to visit him at home. She was considered too young to be a threat.

Around 1970, as Borges and Astete Millán were separating, Kodama ceased being his student, assistant and companion and became his confidant, carer, collaborator and muse. The writer moved back in with his aging mother, now bedbound and unable to speak, for the last three years of her life. According to the official version of the story, Doña Leonor one day brought Kodama's and Borges's hands together over her body.[15]

I was in Argentina to attend a two-week seminar at the Universidad Nacional de San Martín, and to visit the Buenos Aires International Book Fair. During a panel at the latter, I heard Roberto Alifano and Alejandro Vaccaro, Borges's old acquaintances from the Argentine Society of Authors, give their view of Kodama: '*María Kodama es alguien que vive de viuda,*' said Alifano. 'María Kodama is someone who earns a living as a widow.'[16]

Kodama has had long battles with both these men in the Argentine courts and the media. 'Alifano is a rat,' Kodama told me across the table. But she reserved her strongest criticism for her husband's best friend, the writer Adolfo Bioy Casares, who spent much of the 1990s working on a 1600-page compilation of his diary entries about Borges from across their 40-year friendship – to be published only after both men were dead. The book infuriated María Kodama when it finally appeared in 2006. 'María was his love,' Bioy Casares admits, but he expresses doubts that

Borges's feelings were reciprocated. He also says the writer 'lived in fear of making her angry'.[17] Kodama is depicted as a jealous, dominating figure who isolated Borges from his old friends and may even have pressured him to remain in Europe at the end of his life rather than return home.

Speaking to me, her anger focused on the book's alleged inaccuracy and its betrayal of trust: 'I ask you: if a man writes a book in which he invents and distorts your words or puts words in your mouth he doesn't have the courage to say, and he publishes it after you've both died (which is already an act of cowardice, because he doesn't want to take responsibility), if the two of you met in the next world, would you still think that man was your friend?'

I asked her to respond to a few other influential names linked with Borges, starting with the Argentine critic Beatriz Sarlo, a friend in their university days, who has suggested in recent years that Borges's texts will never be properly edited while Kodama is alive: 'That is not an academic judgement, but a personal one that affects my work. I brought a lawsuit against her because we are academic colleagues, and she ought to know the damage that can be caused by unfounded words about someone.'

When I asked her view of leading US Borges scholar Daniel Balderston, she zeroed in on the small fraction of his work that deals with queer themes in Borges's writing. 'Borges was not a homosexual.' Before I could mention any more names, she leaned confidentially across the table, lifting her fringe to show me her slightly swollen and discoloured right eyebrow. 'I keep my hair long to hide it.' Without naming the condition, she told me she has been living with chronic pain for some years, treating it with strong medication. As far as I know she hasn't discussed her ill health publicly. But she brought it up openly with me, knowing I was going to write about our meeting. Kodama insisted her health has not affected her work as director of the Borges Foundation, but admitted it has affected her sleep and her moods. She has said and done some things she regretted and has lost many friends. About the court cases, however, she was unrepentant: 'I have been treated like the wicked witch for defending my husband's legacy…I gave Borges my word that I would take care of his work.' Her soft voice became steely: 'I have been through thirty years of hell. I have been defamed.'

In 1975, journalists photographed Borges weeping at his mother's funeral. His sonnet 'Remorse', written two days later and published in the national newspaper, *La Nación*, remains perhaps his most quoted work in Argentina:

> I have committed the worst sin of all
> That a man can commit. I have not been
> Happy…
> My parents bred and bore me for a higher
> Faith in the human game…
> I let them down. I wasn't happy.[18]

He would later say to Kodama: 'Please don't write anything two days after I die because it is bound to be sentimental and weepy and it will pursue you all your life.'[19]

María Kodama regularly points out that while Borges's complete works from 1923 to 1975 were dedicated to Doña Leonor – 'mother, my very voice. Here we are the two of us, talking'[20] – the texts of his final years were written for her. From around 1973, she began to accompany him abroad on his lecture tours. Invitations from foreign universities, governments and publishers flowed throughout the 1970s and 1980s. Borges's lectures – delivered in a hesitant, stuttering, oracular style – became a significant new strand of his creative output after he lost his sight in 1955. With his blindness he found it impossible to write tightly plotted and densely allusive narratives like those found in the collections *Ficciones* (1944) and *El Aleph* (1949). Increasingly, he focused on poetry, short prose and public lectures.

Kodama and Borges's journeys together through the Americas, Western Europe, Egypt, Turkey, Iceland and Japan are documented in *Atlas* (1984), a travel book pairing Borges's short texts with Kodama's photographs. In 2016, the Borges Foundation put together a travelling exhibition of these photos to commemorate the thirtieth anniversary of Borges's death: the couple placing incense at a Shinto shrine; in sombreros at the base of a Mayan pyramid; in the basket of a hot air balloon about to soar over the Napa Valley vineyards. During their travels, Kodama became his eyes. She discovered he had an enormous visual memory with very clear and detailed recollections of artworks he had seen in European museums as a teenager, and she took to describing the places they visited for his benefit. 'He would always remember a poem related to every place. It was a magical, marvellous relationship.'[21]

In other ways, they were an unusual couple. The two never cohabited and always slept in separate hotel rooms when travelling. In the evenings, she would fold his clothes for the next day and leave them on the end of the bed.

Kodama has told journalists that Borges pestered her to marry him throughout the 1970s, but she always refused, citing the trauma of her parents' separation. She was fearful of being taken over by Borges's 'monstrous fame'. In 1979 – apparently without her knowledge – he made her the primary benefactor of his will. 'If I had known, I would have left him.'[22]

When Borges was diagnosed with liver cancer in late 1984, he refused chemotherapy. To avoid media attention, he elected to keep his condition secret from everyone but María Kodama and his doctor. Not even his sister or his old friend Bioy Casares were told. 'Borges told me he didn't want his death turned into a spectacle and his last breath sold on cassette tape,' Kodama told me. The writer revised the terms of his earlier will, again, Kodama says, without her knowledge. Borges's new will kept her as sole heir to his literary estate, but significantly reduced the cash payout to Epifanía Uveda de Robledo (Fanny), his live-in housekeeper of more than three decades, and the minor provisions made for his sister's children.

On 28 November 1985 Borges and Kodama left Argentina for Europe with permission from the writer's doctor. Kodama believed the purpose of the tour was to say their goodbyes in Italy and Switzerland. But when they arrived in Geneva, Borges said he wanted to stay. 'It was clear to me that he had decided this beforehand, when he learned that he was going to die.'[23] In late December, the couple installed themselves in rooms 308 and 309 of the Hotel l'Arbalète. 'I am a free man,' Borges announced in a statement to the suspicious press. 'I have decided to stay in Geneva, because I associate Geneva with the happiest days of my life.'[24] He had lived in Switzerland with his family during the First World War. For him, it was a place that represented neutrality, privacy and peace. 'The Confederates', the final text in his final collection, takes the creation of the old Swiss confederacy in 1291 as a symbol of his hopes for a world order based on 'forgetting differences and accentuating affinities'.[25] In Geneva, according to Kodama, Borges continued to pressure her on the question of marriage. They had kept their relationship secret for 15 years and he wanted to acknowledge it publicly before he died. He asked his friend Franco Maria Ricci, an Italian editor, to intervene: 'Franco, convince María to marry me; I want to die knowing she's my wife.'

'María, you've been with him since you were young,' the editor said to Kodama. 'It's the only thing that will give him happiness.'[26]

She insisted she was not prepared to become financially dependent on him and compromise her personal freedom. 'You are a prisoner of freedom,' Borges said. In March 1986, she finally relented. Borges ordered his Argentine lawyer to begin the process of seeking a marriage licence in Paraguay – a legal workaround that was necessary because he had separated from but never divorced his first wife. 'My marriage was like the legion of other marriages registered overseas when divorce was not possible in Argentina,' said Kodama. 'It was meant to be a secret between the two of us to make him happy.'[27]

But in May the same year, shortly after the paperwork came through, the news leaked and made headlines in Buenos Aires. Borges died peacefully in his sleep on Saturday

14 June, with Kodama holding his hand. Argentina's most famous agnostic was buried a few plots from John Calvin in Geneva's Plainpalais cemetery. It was not until after Borges was dead, Kodama says, that his lawyers at home called her in Switzerland and told her she was her husband's heir and literary executor.

The period Kodama calls her 'thirty years of hell' began when Borges died. The writer had left his affairs in a mess. The new widow not only had to contend with the grievances of Borges's housekeeper, nephews and the Argentine media, but also the unique editorial difficulties posed by a fragmented oeuvre consisting of hundreds of very short texts.

First came challenges to the validity of the marriage and of Borges's final testament. Borges's housekeeper, Fanny Uveda, and his three nephews claimed Kodama had influenced the elderly writer to change his will. The Argentine courts, however, found that Borges entered willingly into the marriage, and that the union was not even necessary for Kodama to become both the chief beneficiary and the executor of his literary estate.

The widow then embarked on a long series of legal battles of her own, aimed at consolidating her control over all author rights in all languages and combating attacks on her reputation. One target was the North American translator Norman Thomas di Giovanni, with whom Borges had collaborated on some of the best English versions of his work, between 1967 and 1972. After the writer's death, the Borges and di Giovanni versions – for which the translator was receiving a generous 50 per cent of the royalties – were allowed to go out of print. In the 1990s, Penguin commissioned new English versions of Borges's collected works in three hefty volumes. The collected nonfictions are a vital addition to the Borges corpus in English. But most reviewers, myself included, found the new translations of the poetry and fiction inferior to their predecessors. The Penguin editions are now the most widely available version of Borges for English speakers. Kodama also succeeded in blocking di Giovanni from republishing the earlier translations online (though you can still find them if you know where to look). The best English translations of Borges still widely available are those in Yates and Irby's anthology, *Labyrinths*,[28] but the volume contains only a tiny fraction of his total output.

Much of the odium directed towards María Kodama over the years seems really to be aimed at Borges himself. The writer was far from universally admired in Argentina during his lifetime. His stance against the Perón regime, and his opposition to the Cuban Revolution, alienated the left, while his publicly voiced doubts about the Argentine people's readiness for democracy, and his support for military dictatorships at home and in Chile (later retracted) probably cost him the Nobel Prize. Borges's decision to die abroad only reinforced the image some of his countrymen have of him as a reactionary snob. Even today, everyone in Argentina has an opinion about Borges. 'Why are you foreigners so obsessed with him?' scolded the chatty manager of my hotel. 'He wasn't even an Argentine writer. He was a European writer.'

Kodama has tried to combat this perception by

emphasising the importance of the writer's hometown to his creative output during the commemorations of the thirtieth anniversary of his death. 'Borges, like the ancient Greeks, belonged to his city...He was born in Buenos Aires and Buenos Aires was his very being.'[29]

Borges's Buenos Aires, however, was the expanding port city of the 1880s and 1890s reimagined from the vantage point of the 1920s and 1930s. It's hard to find any trace of it today. The house at 994 on the calle Maipu, where the writer was born in 1899, is an apartment complex now, with a small commemorative plaque beside the door. Though the Palermo street where Borges spent most of his childhood, the old calle Serrano, has been renamed in his honour, the house where the family lived in those years – a few blocks south of the Plaza Italia – has been demolished and replaced by a rundown bar. The old national library in San Telmo, where Borges was director between 1955 and 1973, is in urgent need of renovation, though it still hosts the national institutes of contemporary dance and musicology.

Meanwhile, the Borges Museum at 1660 on the calle Anchorena in Recoleta, which doubles as the headquarters of Kodama's international foundation, has only a tenuous connection to the writer's life (Borges and his mother lived next door for a few years in the 1940s). One of Kodama's assistants told me that the foundation has been trying to buy the adjacent building back from the neighbours for years: 'But the señora doesn't want to sell.'

The regionalist 'Borges of Buenos Aires' exists in tension with the cosmopolitan fabulist who is read around the world in dozens of languages. In 2016, in addition to the commemorations in Argentina, María Kodama presided over similar ceremonies in Switzerland, Spain and New York. 'All of these events demonstrate that his work remains alive,' she says.[30] The process of monumentalising Borges in brass, stone and deluxe editions, now 30 years advanced, contrasts markedly with the writer's own sly prediction of his place in literary history. The epilogue to the original 1974 Emecé edition of his Spanish *Obras Completas* takes the form of an apocryphal 2074 encyclopedia entry. The 'author and autodidact' 'José Borges', we are told, is mainly remembered for never having written a novel.[31]

Among scholars, the most serious complaint about the way the foundation has managed the writer's legacy is that there is no proper critical edition of Borges in his own language. I asked Kodama whether such an edition will ever appear. 'I have heard that question many times and I ask you who is the person capable of editing a critical edition of Borges? I am willing to review people's qualifications.' Ultimately, Kodama says, she does not know of anyone she would trust with the job. For the time being, the scholarly apparatus in the Spanish editions of Borges compares badly with what is available for most classic twentieth-century authors.

This needn't have been the case. The publisher Sudamericana, owned by Penguin Random House, outbid Borges's old publisher Emecé for the worldwide rights to his work at the 2010 Frankfurt Bookfair. News reports suggest they paid close to 2 million euros.[32] But the 2011 Sudamericana edition, the version I own, was a missed opportunity to produce a quality, integral Borges for the twenty-first century. It simultaneously respects and ignores the author's wishes. Many of the early texts have been extensively rewritten by the older Borges, who grew to dislike his youthful style, but there are no notes to indicate the changes. In the same edition, three early books of essays the writer suppressed entirely during his lifetime are republished in their original form. It is almost impossible to trace the development of Borges's style and ideas using this or any other edition because none of them offer even the most minimal explanation of the chaotic, unchronological sequencing of the collected texts. Kodama herself acknowledges that the other main Spanish-language option on the market, the 2009 Emecé critical edition, is really only an annotated edition. The notes are manifestly inadequate for the purpose of scholarship.

Unfortunately for English and Spanish speakers, the best version of Borges in any language is the French *Oeuvres Complètes* published by Gallimard. The second edition was delayed for ten years as Kodama sued Borges's old friend, the editor Jean-Pierre Bernés. She eventually succeeded in forcing him to hand over copies of recordings he had made while collaborating with Borges in 1986 on the notes for the first edition. As a result of this falling out, non-French speakers are unlikely to be able to access Borges and Bernés's extensive notes any time soon.

More recently, Kodama has used the financial resources and institutional power of the estate to pursue young experimental writers, such as the Spaniard Agustín Fernández Mallo and the Argentine Pablo Katchadjian, who have creatively appropriated Borges's writing. Katchadjian faced the possibility of up to six years of jail time and a US$80,000 fine for publishing 150 copies of *El Aleph Engordado* (*The Fattened Aleph*), his novella-length expansion

of Borges's famous story, through a tiny Argentine independent publisher.[33] Legitimate artistic practice or a violation
of intellectual property? Either way, the case more or less
destroyed whatever goodwill was left towards Kodama
among the younger generation of Spanish-speaking writers
and intellectuals.

From the window of the cafe, a slab of blue sky was visible
between the roofs of the grey and brown apartment towers
of Recoleta. As lunchtime approached, I was coming to the
end of my three-page list of questions. But Kodama showed
no signs of impatience or boredom.

'What do you miss about Borges?'

'He is inside me. I feel he accompanies me spiritually and
that he has given me the strength to fight for all these years.
Yes, I miss the way we had fun together.'

'As you grow older, what motivates you to keep promoting Borges's work so energetically through the foundation?'

'This has been my job for thirty years. You only give your
life to something if you love it madly. If I didn't love him
madly, I wouldn't do it.'

Others have asked Kodama what will happen to the
estate when she dies. Her answer rarely changes – 'Why
would you ask me that? I plan to live for two hundred
years'[34] – so I didn't ask. Though the conversation often
drifted back to Borges, I had learned many things about her
over the last three hours: that she cannot cook; that she used
to like horseriding and dancing flamenco, but nowadays
prefers to meditate and read; that she sleeps only five hours
a night; that she is so dispirited by Argentine politics that
she has not opened a newspaper since the year 2000. She

hasn't been able to face them since she read about the great Argentine cardiologist René Favaloro – one of the pioneers of coronary bypass surgery – at the time of the Argentine financial crisis. With his research foundation in financial trouble, and the country itself about to default on its foreign debt, Favaloro had shot himself in the heart.

'He could have gone anywhere, this man. But he chose to stay in this country...' She shook her head. She was expressing the sense of frustration and wasted potential one routinely encounters talking to Argentines of all social classes about their country. Hearing her speak this way, I thought she was every bit as much a product of this place as the exhausted-looking waiter and the chess-playing hobo.

We continued chatting for ten minutes after my questions ran out. Leaving the café, we discussed the pleasure of reading aloud for someone you love – a habit we had in common. I told her my wife and I were reading *Fortunata y Jacinta* by the great nineteenth-century Spanish realist Benito Pérez Galdós, in a beautiful hand-me-down edition her parents had brought us from Mexico as a wedding present. The book had belonged to R's blind aunt, whose mother helped her complete her literature thesis by reading aloud for her. It was full of mysterious page separators with notes written in braille. María Kodama liked the sound of that.

I asked her, before we parted, which of the books she used to read aloud for Borges she most enjoyed sharing with him. 'I liked to read for him in Greek,' she said. Kodama studied ancient Greek at university; Borges never had. 'He always said he envied the fact I could read Greek. And I would say, "Borges, let me have this one thing."' *The Iliad* was their favourite. He knew many passages from Homer so well he could follow the gist though he didn't speak the language. Kodama quoted a passage to me in Greek, there on the sunny corner of Corrientes and Juncal – a scene that was often in her thoughts in Geneva while Borges was dying. A brief Spanish gloss, another kiss on the cheek, and she was gone.

It wasn't until several weeks later, back in Australia, that I had a chance to look up the passage. I found it in book six of *The Iliad*, in my copy of Fagles's translation. When Andromache follows Hector to the gates of Troy, with their baby son in her arms, she begs him not to return to the battlefield because she has already lost her mother, father and seven brothers, and he is her only surviving family. This was the passage María Kodama recited to me as we parted:

> You, Hector – you are my father now, my noble mother
> a brother too, and you are my husband, young and warm
> and strong!
> Pity me, please! Take your stand on the rampart here,
> before you orphan your son and make your wife a widow.[35]

San Miguel del Monte

The horizon always undefined…[1]

– Domingo Faustino Sarmiento

At last I spied my old friend Benjamín Ortega squinting through the gloom from the far side of the bar.

'Ben!' I flagged him down.

'¡*Australiano*! It's four o'clock in the afternoon and you're already drinking?'

'We're here for the game.'

The Puerta Roja was full of Buenos Aires hipsters and foreign backpackers drinking craft beer, watching the football on a giant projection screen. The *superclásico*, Boca versus River, is the biggest rivalry in Argentine football. It's something like Collingwood–Carlton with a genuine risk of fans killing each other. Ben embraced R, kissed both cheeks.

'The famous *Mexicana*.'

'The famous *Argentino*.'

'You've cut off all your hair,' he said, turning back to me. 'You look like a bank manager.'

'We're getting older.'

'Speak for yourself.'

Ben has 10 or 15 years on me, I think, but I'll never know for sure.

'You can't ask a middle-aged woman her age,' he scolded when I once discreetly inquired. He was overdressed for the grungy bar in a navy-blue turtleneck, cream-coloured slacks and expensive-looking brown leather shoes. His hair was streaked with grey, he had salt-and-pepper stubble on his cheeks, and he was a little heavier around the chops than nine years back. His cheeky smile retained the ability to make rudeness charming.

'What's this slop you're eating?'

'Quesadillas.'

'In Buenos Aires? Ay, *Australiano*. This Mexican girl's ruined you.'

We ordered a round of drinks to ease the flow of memories: beers for R and me, soda water for Ben.

'These Australians are barbarians with their drinking in the afternoon,' he said to her. 'I see you've fallen under his bad influence.'

'We're on holidays.' She smiled.

The match was tense, defensive. Just before half-time, one of the Boca strikers tumbled dramatically to the grass in the penalty area. When he slotted home his kick, the crowd in the bar erupted.

'How on earth did you end up with such a responsible job, Ben?' I shouted over the din. 'I can't believe they let you organise anything.'

It had taken at least a dozen attempts via email, social media and text message to arrange our meeting. Yet he was obviously highly capable in his professional life. A high-school history teacher when last I saw him, he was now a senior public servant with the municipal government in San Miguel del Monte, two hours south of the capital.

'Ah, you're still busting my balls about 2007.'

Ben reads English perfectly well but prefers to limit his spoken language to 'fuck you' and 'you're busting my balls', insults he hurled at me daily, smiling cheerfully, when I was teaching for him at the agricultural college in Monte. I'd agreed to work for free on the understanding the school would provide meals and a homestay with a local family. But for the first six weeks he had me sharing a dormitory with a dozen smelly teenage boys.

'You should have heard how this First World princess complained,' he said, appealing to R.

'I didn't expect the Buenos Aires Hilton, I just wanted him to organise what the contract promised. I had to stage a protest in his classroom.'

'A protest! It was an illegal occupation,' complained Ben. 'One day I arrived to teach my morning class and all the kids were laughing. He'd dragged his mattress into the room and was lying there snoring.'

'I was inspired by you Argentines, with all your blockades and sit-ins. Anyway, you persuaded Camila to let me have her spare room pretty quickly after that.'

He rolled his eyes. 'Your husband's a real ballbuster.'

The moment R disappeared to the bathroom he filled me in on an old girlfriend. 'She married the Fernández boy: the chubby one who plays the accordion. They had a baby girl last year.'

'I'm glad she's well. What about old Leonard Barton? I wrote him a couple of letters, but he never replied. Probably got lost in the post.'

'They sold the house by the lake when the señora died. Last I heard he was living with his daughter. His health was very bad.'

When Ben left briefly to make a call, R asked if he had a partner.

'I don't know nowadays. He used to have a thing with the chemistry teacher. I forget his name.'

'*His* name?'

'Yes, a few of the other teachers knew, but not the principal. Monte's a small town. They'd catch separate buses to and from BA on weekends to be together in secret.'

I remembered Ben telling me he'd run for local council in his thirties. It looked like he had a real chance early in the campaign. Handsome and articulate, he had the backing of all his students' parents and his thoughtful columns for the local newspaper were winning supporters around town. An anonymous phone call put an end to it.

'They threatened to tell his boss if he didn't withdraw,' I told R. 'Silvia was very Catholic, so were a lot of the parents.'

'I wonder if he's still with the chemistry teacher?' R whispered as Ben reappeared.

We didn't get a chance to ask.

'Did I tell you Mamá died?' he said, sitting down again. We still occasionally emailed or chatted, but this news hadn't reached me.

'No. I'm sorry, Ben.'

'Late last year. She was ninety-two.'

I remembered a stooped woman at a backyard *asado*, who'd kissed me on both cheeks, making the sign of the cross in the smoky air. Ben had lived with her all his life.

'I'm with my sister's family now – I'm the *tío solterón*.'

We kept to the surface after that, reminiscing and teasing each other. The second half of the *superclásico* fizzled to a one-all draw and the bar emptied out.

'So, you'll come see us next weekend and stay with Camila?' Ben asked as we walked him to the bus stop.

'I think we'll just come for the day. We don't want to be an inconvenience.'

'Fuck you, *Australiano*,' he said, patting me on the cheek. 'Three visits in nine years and you won't even stay the night? You have to stay.'

At the end of my question mark–shaped loop around South America in 2007, I found peace in Monte for six months. Camila and her 16-year-old son, Carlos, took me into their home and made me feel part of the family, the school paying a small stipend for my upkeep.

It was good to be working again. Ben had me teaching small-group remedial workshops to students who'd failed English multiple times. Most were teenage boys, the sons of farmers and abattoir workers. They were great guitar players and folk dancers, but didn't see any value in learning a language beyond impressing girls with a few English pop songs.

'Why should I speak English?' said Santiago. 'The English blew my Dad's hand off in the Malvinas.'

I bet Santiago and his friends that I could get them to speak English for a whole hour, without reverting to Spanish, by the end of term.

'Let's put a hundred pesos on it,' he said.

'You're on.'

In spring, I fell hard for a local girl, the mechanic's daughter. Every weekend I would stay with her in her tiny flat in the university city of La Plata, two hours away. She was studying to be a psychoanalyst. Wherever I went in the world, I was surrounded by psychologists. In La Plata, the avocado tree dropped its fruit on the roof in the evenings. I'd climb the drainpipe next morning and collect one for our breakfast. From the rooftop, I imagined the clouds were maps of countries we might visit together.

Those plains again, treeless and unrippling, scrolling by the bus window. The pampa in the purple dusk quietens the mind; it has the flatness of the sea on a still day.

'Tell me we're not going all the way out here to see your ex-girlfriend,' said R in the mini-van to Monte. All day she'd been complaining of an upset stomach.

'No, we're going to see Ben and Camila.'

'And if we run into her in the street?'

'We'll say hello and move on.'

Camila flagged the van down on the main road into town. She was in her fifties now, but had the same long black fringe, bright-red lipstick and hoop earings.

'Shames!' She kissed me on both cheeks, did the same for R. 'I stopped the bus because I thought you probably wouldn't remember how to find the house from the centre of town. Do you still get lost?'

'Not as often as I used to.'

'All the time,' said R.

Camila led us past the funeral parlour and the florist, important reference points as few of the streets have names.

'People in Monte gossiped when he came to stay with us because he bought me flowers,' Camila told R. 'In small towns, people have big mouths. They said, "Camila Sorrentino is living with a man twenty years younger than her, he must be a gigolo."'

'And what did you say, señora?'

'I told them he was my *per-so-nal tr-ainer.*' She said it in English, smacking her lips, strutting a little for effect.

They'd paved the Sorrentinos' nameless street since my last visit. Camila's three-bedroom brick house was identical out front, but in the backyard they'd converted her ex-husband's furniture workshop into a massage parlour. Her daughter Paola worked there part-time while Camila took the baby.

Paola wore dark eyeliner and a nose ring; she had a skull tattooed on one shoulder, a rose on the other.

'This is Rodrigo,' she said, passing me her pink-cheeked 18-month-old for a cuddle.

'*Hola, pequeñín.*'

'Don't ask about his papá. His papá is an arsehole.'

'Not the Patagonian heavy metal drummer?'

'No, a different arsehole. A later one.'

Camila showed R a photograph of me outside the house nine years earlier with her son Carlos. Her living room cabinet was mostly filled with his motorcross trophies and school medallions, but she pointed out a shelf set aside for the Christmas presents I sent every few years to maintain the link. I was embarrassed to see so many tea towels adorned with kitsch Australiana.

'It's a shame Carlos isn't here,' she said. 'He's in Brazil with his girlfriend now. They run a hostel at the beach. Somebody gave him the idea of being a traveller right as he was finishing high school.'

'Sorry about that.'

In the evening, Ben came by with pizzas and empanadas and we talked until late. He teased us relentlessly about our Mexican accents, dropping in and out of his Speedy Gonzales impersonation:

'Say *ahorita*, say *andale*.'

'At least I don't use pretentious words like *vertiginosamente* in every article I write.'

'But isn't it true, *Australiano*? Don't you think that time passes vertiginously?'

'Yes, it's true.'

One thing that hadn't changed was the instability of the Argentine economy: groceries were up 30 or 40 per cent on last year. I asked Paola and Camila how the most recent round of inflation had affected them.

'We're lucky,' Paola said. 'The water comes up to our neck sometimes, but it always goes down again. A lot of people are under water.'

Camila grilled R about upcoming plot twists in her favourite Mexican soap opera, which she watched daily as she cared for her grandson.

'He's the dearest little thing. Do you think you'll have kids soon?'

'We're not sure,' said R.

'Not sure if you want to?'

'Not sure if we can,' I replied. 'The specialist said there's a less than five per cent chance.'

We eventually relented to Ben's bullying and agreed to spend the night in Carlos's old room. Camila hadn't changed anything since he left. The walls were plastered with Ramones posters and the bookshelf was full of dirt-bike magazines.

'She really misses him,' said R from the darkness beside me in the cramped single bed.

'She does.'

'I'm glad we came in the end. I'm glad I got to meet your old friends.'

'They're special people.'

'They're great. They're so different to people in the city.'

'It's a different country out here.' I held her tightly. 'You don't feel sick anymore?'

'No, I feel better.'

As we drifted off to sleep in the little brick house on the pampa, I felt the earth tilt and shudder. It could have been a distant tremor out west in the Andes, or just a faint vibration passing from her body into mine.

One clear, warm morning in November 2007, I flicked all the way to page 52 of *La Nación* to find the results of the Australian federal election: '*Gana el partido laborista en Australia.*' The Labor Party had finally won government. Not long afterwards, my mother called to tell me Al had suffered a series of small strokes.

'I don't think he should be living on his own anymore,' she said on the phone.

I told the school I was leaving for good and the mechanic's daughter that I'd be back. It was my fault the romance dragged on for months by phone, delaying the inevitable and causing unnecessary pain. Eventually, on her analyst's advice, she took the iniative and ended things, and I set out for outback Queensland trying to forget her.

The big box of Spanish books that I shipped home from Monte contained the beginnings of my library of Latin American literature, which I have added to with each subsequent journey, so that ten years of my life are now chronicled there: language textbooks and Argentine classics; everything ever written about the Australian Utopians in Paraguay; the dark green spine of Gabo's opus; and finally an unbroken run of Mexican authors.

During my final month in Monte, my old travel buddy Valentina emailed out of the blue to ask if she could visit. We sat in the soft grass by the lagoon at midday on a Saturday, drinking mate, watching a pair of teenage fisherman haul in carp and hurl them back. Poor Valentina. By now her hair was a tangled mess like mine. Her clothes were filthy, and she was as thin as Corina.

'Sorry to land on you like this,' she said. 'I'm broke.'

After Bolivia, she'd hitchhiked through the Chaco swamplands in the north of Paraguay. She told me she'd run out of cash between towns and needed to beg food from villagers who barely had enough for themselves. She was struck down by a stomach bug and nursed back to health by a *campesino* family. When she was strong enough to hitch to Asunción and see a doctor, she discovered her travel insurance had lapsed, and she couldn't afford the treatment.

Her parents, of course, had bailed her out.

'What will you do now?'

'I was wondering if you could lend me some money to tide me over?'

'You've got to be joking, Valentina.'

'I'm sorry to ask.'

'I can get you free accommodation for a week. That's the best I can do. And you'll have to earn it by doing some teaching.'

Ben agreed to let her pitch her tent in his classroom overnight so long as she was out of the way by first period and stayed no longer than a week. She stayed a fortnight in the end, but earned her keep, teaching five hours a day. At first she was shy, but soon her posture improved and her voice became audible from the back row. Santiago and the other Argentine boys, to my astonishment, were smitten with Valentina. They obsessed over her huge green eyes and French accent, calling her the *'profe belga'*.

'If you want to ask her out, you'll have to speak English,' I lied, 'because she doesn't know any Spanish at all.'

On her final day, they all clambered to sign her shirt in the language they'd sworn never to learn: 'Marry me... Here's my number...I'll never forget you.'

I never claimed my 100 pesos.

'Where to next?' I asked Valentina at the bus station. 'Easter Island? Antarctica?'

'Brussels,' she said. 'It's definitely time.'

The Lakeside House

You will come here all your life for renewal.[1]

– Judith Wright

The pale oval of R's face turns to me in darkness.

'Look, she's dreaming.'

The baby's cheek settles into my chest and her lashes flutter against my skin. Her breathing slows to match mine. Soon, it has the soft insistence of faraway surf. I whisper so as not to wake her.

'Did you dream?'

'We were in Mexico,' says R. 'All my aunts and uncles came to meet Vera. But it was our Brisbane house.'

My mouth is parched, my water bottle empty at the bedside. February heat broods behind the closed curtains; morning surges and builds. Wind-stirred branches, trilling birds, shore-break lapping the lake's edge. My father's voice (which is my voice) carries from across the water. He's taken my in-laws out in the canoe. We hear laughter, splashing oars, a confused medley of Spanish and English. The two sides of our lives commingle in the sultry air.

'I don't remember if I dreamed.'

'You never remember.'

The three of us doze until lunchtime, until sweat pools between Vera's beating heart and mine. I wake to find R has parted the curtains a crack, returned to bed. Her hands, folded over the still-raw caesarean scar, rise and fall with her breathing. By reflected light that ripples the ceiling, I drift back to sleep reading a collection of Judith Wright's letters and poems to her husband Jack McKinney: 'So, perilously joined / lighted in one small room, / we have made all things true.'[2]

This little town was a place of peaceful repose for Judith, Jack and their daughter Meredith, as it's been for my parents since I was a boy. In my dreams, I show Vera through its streets.

Judith Wright holidayed regularly at Boreen Point in the Sunshine Coast Hinterland from 1953 until Jack McKinney's death in 1966. Many of her poems from this particularly tense period of the Cold War express fear of atomic extinction from the perspective of a new parent:

> Bombs ripen on the leafless tree
> under which the children play.
> And there my darling all alone
> dances in the spying day.[3]

We were feeling a bit like that over the summer of 2017, with the Trump inauguration shortly after our daughter's birth, a new round of nuclear brinksmanship on the Korean peninsula, and R's ecologist colleagues publishing a paper most weeks on how quickly the planet is cooking. To make matters worse, South-East Queensland sweltered in the mid- to high thirties from November through March. We were lucky to be able to retreat to my parents' breezy lakeside weekender a couple of hours north of Brisbane. Re-reading Wright's Cooloola poems from *The Gateway* (1953) to *The Other Half* (1966) over that long, hot Queensland summer, it was hard not to hear echoes of our own anxious times. Wright's lyrics from the shore of Lake Cootharaba are powerfully infused with what the contemporary Australian philosopher Glenn Albrecht calls *solastalgia*, the distress caused by negative changes in the home environment.[4] These poems find local correlates – sand mining, and deforestation at Cooloola during Joh Bjelke-Petersen's reign – for a planetary-scale ecological crisis that was then only beginning to be understood.

Nowadays, Boreen Point has a population of about 300, which swells during the spring sailing regatta and the summer holidays. There is money here, half an hour's drive from the upscale beach resort at Noosa Heads. But it expresses itself in a sleepy, unshowy way. Up the hillside, eccentric timber houses of two and three storeys jostle for the best lake view. Built up high to guard against flooding, they all look vaguely like stranded boats. And, indeed, catamarans and canoes are drawn up on many lawns in front of lush gardens of bromelias and ferns. The streets have quaint, bucolic names: Orchard Avenue, Vista Street. Most locals are past retirement age: aside from a couple of tradies taking advantage of the cheap rent, anyone under fifty is on holiday. Everybody is white.

211

My parents' lakeside house is a 1940s Queenslander built with local cedar from the sawmill days before the national park. It's painted to match the blues and greys of the lake by changing light, and it's furnished with my maternal grandfather's things. Like the house, the Parker dining set is a postwar classic: a dark hardwood table and sturdy black vinyl-covered chairs. The CD collection is all Naxos classics and Yankee jazz bands from the 1930s and 1940s.

When Al died, Mum and Dad put the modest inheritance towards a deposit on the house. I inherited his bad posture and social awkwardness. I'm drafting this slouched at the mahogany writing desk where he used to keep journals and letters from his old air-force buddies.

'Melaleuca', the little yellow cottage Judith and Jack once owned, is a couple of blocks up the hill from Mum and Dad's place. Though still occupied, it looks rather forlorn: the tin letterbox rusted; the once-pink terrace faded grey, cracking at the edges; the concrete plaster facade half hidden behind the banksia bush where green rosella hop from twig to twig.

In the spring of 1953, when Meredith was four, the couple left their home on Mount Tamborine and drove north for the Noosa Lakes, hunting wildflowers. In the hinterland, they stumbled on 'a little village of nine or ten houses and a general store', as Judith wrote in her autobiography, 'all delectably perched on a lake shore above a pink and white sandstone cliff'.[5] Most of the residents were fishermen or timber workers in those days, but one local man of fortune was building cheap holiday cottages. His method was to construct a house frame of sawmill timber and dig a trench around it, using the dug-out sand to build the cement walls.

The couple put down a deposit on one of the prototypes, then 'scratched and scraped and sold and blackmailed the Bank for an overdraught'.[6]

That 'light-filled concrete house' became their refuge for many years. With no electricity and no sealed roads, it was a perfect retreat for two writers: 'Solid, warm, and comforting...the blue of the lake shone through its windows.'[7] It was there on the shores of Lake Cootharaba that little Meredith learned to swim and many of the best poems of Judith Wright's middle career were written.

Who'd have thought a house made of sand could outlive its occupants.

Old Al, to whom we owe the lakeside house, was only a few years younger than Judith Wright. I thought of him often as I re-read her poetry that summer, not so much because of the surface correspondences – both were born between wars, both went deaf as young adults – but because he was the person of her generation to whom I've been closest. On reflection, the two seemed to embody contrary impulses in postwar Australia: the desire to change everything; the need to reassert order.

Meredith McKinney wrote in a memoir of her parents that her memories of the couple were 'overwhelmingly of them reading together'.[8] Like Judith and Jack, Old Al wasn't physically demonstrative. His poor hearing, a result of the roaring engines of Lancaster bombers, could make him seem withdrawn. But he was affectionate in his stiff, masculine way. I remember a patient ping-pong coach and a clever leg-spin bowler; a cautious, thrifty, round-shouldered old man, who labelled his margarine with a marker in case the expiry date wore off. I was too young to grasp that his need for routine and his odd habits might have something to do with his war service. Some Second World War pilots peed on their plane's tailwheel for good luck before every sortie or wore the same shoes every flight.[9] When they returned to civilian life, they often developed other compulsive behaviours. Even as a boy, I wanted to understand why it was so important for Al's lunch to be on the table before midday and for the lawn of his villa to be perfectly even.

I have especially vivid memories of the two of us spending a lot of time together the year before I left for South America, while my parents were overseas. I was his most frequent visitor, aside from the Veterans' Affairs nurse who came daily to change his bandages around 11. On most occasions, he'd take me for a soggy buffet lunch at the RSL and tell the same three or four terse, elliptical stories about the war. There was always a good deal of technical detail about how to read the instruments in the cockpit, and nothing at all about how it feels to be shot at.

One day, he felt dizzy before lunch and the nurse put him to bed. Rifling through his things, I uncovered dozens of old journals. I hoped I'd find intense emotions like Meredith McKinney discovered in her mother's love letters. Finally, I'd know the full story of the New York blonde who gave him his first taste of Coca-Cola in Times Square in 1940; how he felt about the fire-bombing of Dresden; why he read atheist tract after atheist tract, as if to shore up his disbelief.

I was disappointed. There was nothing in the journals but hundreds of 'To Do' lists: 'buy milk', 'pay car insurance', 'birthday card for Kath'.

Serves me right for snooping, I thought, slumping in his armchair and listening to him snore.

'How come you never march on Anzac Day?' I asked when he woke up.

'Why make a fuss?' he replied.

Judith and Jack always made a fuss. They met in Brisbane, in 1944, through the circle around Clem Christesen's new literary quarterly, *Meanjin*. The magazine published writers of 'strong socio-political consciousness'[10] who saw the end of the war as an opportunity for progressive social change. Beyond contributing to the journal, they were living that change: she was 29; he was 53 – and married.

'You and I are queer and sinful fish,' she wrote to him at Easter 1945 from her family's pastoral property near Armidale.[11] Like her contemporaries Patrick White and Geoffrey Dutton, Judith Wright hailed from the old squattocracy, a complicated heritage that fed both her intense feeling for the Australian landscape and her distaste for the materialism of Australian society.

'I can feel that nineteenth-century atmosphere,' Jack replied, 'and how strange our life would seem by contrast. We of course are right, but it's difficult being the only people who are right.'[12]

Judith's father wept when she told him of the relationship. Because Jack's wife refused divorce, they were unable to marry until years later, in 1962, when no-fault divorce had become legal. And, since his meagre pension was dedicated to the upkeep of his four children, Judith had to take on the role of economic provider.

'I am really an awkward proposition for you to handle,' he acknowledged in an early letter.[13]

But by then, Judith was in love.

Not long after we met, R told me she was about to go to Mexico for three months.

'I'll be doing fieldwork in the cloud forest and I don't know if I'll be able to stay in touch.'

We were introduced by a mutual friend in 2009 when we were both postgraduates at the University of Queensland. That first balmy Brisbane night, we talked until dawn on a West End balcony, and woke on our friend's couch next morning to talk some more.

While she was away, I wrote her long emails describing my efforts to keep possums out of my shabby studio apartment at St Lucia. Every few days, I'd receive a reply from remote villages in Oaxaca, where she and her volunteers were wading about in gumboots, catching frogs and nipping off their toes above the first knuckle for DNA sequencing in the laboratory. Her life sounded like an adventure I wanted to join. She told me about eating tadpole soup with hospitable Zapotec *campesinos*, and about hearing a jaguar roar in the bushes beside camp.

On her first night back in Brisbane, I cooked her dinner and gifted her a yellow ukulele. We were inseparable after that.

Jack was recovering from a breakdown when he met Judith. He was a First World War pensioner who'd fought in France and still suffered from shellshock. Judith remarked to her biographer Veronica Brady that she could always tell when he was having an attack because 'he turned pale and sweaty and his eyes would go away'.[14] Eking a living from the land during the Depression had wrecked his health, and the outbreak of the second war sent him into a mental spiral that accelerated the breakdown of his first marriage. When he met Judith, he was a self-described 'pensioner-gardener, hangeron-handyman'[15] who lived alone in a shack at Surfers Paradise. On weekends, he visited the Christesens in Brisbane to borrow books from their well-stocked library. Jack was in the process of refashioning himself as a 'wild philosopher without a degree'.[16] He read madly to catch up on all he'd missed and began work on an ambitious treatise which tried to explain the crisis in Western thought that had led to the world wars and the development of nuclear weapons.

Judith was attracted to his arguments. She, too, felt that there had been 'a sort of hypertrophy of the intellectual side of Western man at the expense of the feeling side'.[17] But she was worldly enough to recognise that his knowledge had been cobbled together. Through her administrative job at the University of Queensland, she provided him with books and articles on the latest developments in physics and contemporary philosophy, which Jack devoured gratefully as he embarked on his epic.

'My Darling we're going to be very happy and defy the world,' he wrote to her.[18]

'I have doubts about this Jack,' I said to R, laying the collection of their letters on the bed beside me.

'¿Por qué?'

'I understand everyone felt they owed a debt to old soldiers. And I know that women were expected to keep house in those days. But it really seems to me he got the better end of the deal.'

'She was in love with him.'

'I find even his love letters unreadable. Let alone the philosophy. Listen to this…' I read her a tangled parsing of Hegel he'd sent Judith during one of his manic bursts of reading.

'Well, I don't claim to understand what he's talking about, but I'm not a philosopher.'

'Nor am I. But my point is he got to sit there for fifteen years writing his unreadable book, while she typed it for him, paid the bills, became the leading Australian poet of her generation, and did all the housework.'

I expected her to agree. In fact, I was probably overstating my case to impress her. But she was adamant in her defence of Jack.

'She was in love with him,' she said again, as if that explained everything.

R and I soon moved in together on Ryan Street near the river. The UQ Ecology Lab was flush with money in those days and attracted brilliant young people from all over the world. I grew accustomed to Friday night dinners at the Asian places along Hardgrave Road with a dozen or more nationalities at our table. Often, I was the only Australian and found myself cast in the enjoyable role of local expert.

Soon, she took me to meet her parents in Mexico City. They were friendly, but cautious. Why did this Australian speak Spanish with a thick Argentine accent? How serious was he about their daughter?

During the same trip, R took me hiking in the Oaxacan sierra near her field sites. For three days, we tramped the high ridge lines of forested hills, watching vultures circle over fields of yellowish maize. Eventually, in a dusty mountain outpost, we came upon a woman no taller than a child, standing in waist-high grass. A wooden pail half-filled with herbs dangled from the crook of her arm. In her free hand, she brandished a scythe. She invited us to her hut and offered to perform a *limpia*, a cleansing ceremony – for a small fee. She had me strip to my boxer shorts so she could rub my bare chest with coarse, freshly cut herbs dipped in alcohol. She murmured Spanish and Zapotec incantations. She blew on the dampness over my heart until it dried. Her two long plaits were the colour of ashes, but her skin was as smooth as polished stone. When her huge yellow eyes gazed into mine, I felt she intuited things about R and me that we were hiding from ourselves and each other: that our wedding bands were only for the sake of appearances; that we weren't ready to commit because we were still too unsure of ourselves as individuals to love one another well; that only a painful rupture would teach us how to be together – to risk open dialogue, to listen across languages, to live with difference. But perhaps the chain of impressions I attributed to the woman was no more than a projection of my own fears. Perhaps in her culture the little frown she made as she stared into my face opened onto some other unimaginable hinterland of feeling. Or perhaps, like most fortune tellers, she was simply trying to guess what her customers most wanted to hear. In the end, instead of revealing the hidden truth of our relationship, she merely restoked the woodfire stove with a poker. Turning back to us, she muttered, 'You and your wife will have a daughter.'

We carry Vera down to the strand to admire the iridescent green plumage of the ducks. Nice to think of little Meredith McKinney 'running ecstatically'[19] into the same calm, brown waters.

A little distance off, her Australian and Mexican grand-parents are paddling the big red canoe with her aunt alongside in the kayak, translating. It's lovely to see them enjoying each other's company. Vera's *abuelos* flew thousands of kilometres to be in Australia for her birth, only to sweat through the hottest Queensland summer in memory. They spent much of it in the kitchen of our cramped rental house in East Brisbane with the oven and stove cranked. When not stocking the deep freezer with hand-made corn tortillas and spicy chipotle creations for us to eat after they'd left, they took long walks around Brisbane's mostly treeless inner south. Often, they returned from Woolloongabba, Coorparoo or Stones Corner laden with heavy shopping bags when the sun blazed overhead.

One especially hot day, we had to take Vera's *abuelo* to the emergency ward with chest pains.

'His heart's fine,' said the doctor. 'But we're going to have to get some electrolytes into him. He's severely dehydrated.'

Back in the stuffy little kitchen, we decided they'd worked enough. It was time to get out of the city.

'Why don't we all go to the lake?' suggested my parents. 'There's enough space for everyone.'

Squatting in the sugar-fine sand, I dangle Vera's feet in the cool shallows.

From the end of the wooden pier we gaze across the lake's choppy brown water. This whole sweep of beaches, dunes, mangroves, swamps, woodlands and waterways – from

Tin Can Bay down to Noosa – is named after the coastal sand cypress.[20] Sometimes the sea breeze in the branches sings the name of the country: Coo-loo-la.

There were probably fewer than 1000 Aboriginal people here before 1788. The early British weren't impressed. 'Nothing...can well be imagined more barren than this peninsula,' wrote Matthew Flinders in 1802.[21] Infertile, sandy soils have kept the human population down, but Cooloola teems with other forms of life: king parrots, black cockatoos and the red-backed fairy wren that once brought the sun's fire to earth; echidnas, bandicoots and flying foxes; dugong, ghost crabs and bream; eucalypts, goat's foot vine and the phaius orchid of Judith Wright's lyric:

> For whose eyes – for whose eyes
> does this blind being weave
> sand's poverty, water's sour,
> the white and black of the hour
> into the image I hold
> and cannot understand?[22]

Over the eastern shoreline looms the largest vegetated dune system in the world, which has served as a navigational aid for generations of watercraft: bark canoes, colonial sloops, pleasure sailors' catamarans and fishermen's tin runabouts. From its source in the mountains, the tea-coloured black waters of the Noosa River meander slowly south through a chain of six saltwater lakes: Cooloola, Como, Cootharaba, Cooroibah, Doonella and Weyba.

Cootharaba, our lake, is the largest – about 10 kilometres long and 5 kilometres wide. In Gubbi Gubbi, the name means place of trees whose wood makes sturdy clubs. Down by the pier is a stone monument to Eliza Fraser, the shipwrecked white woman who survived with local Indigenous people for several months in 1836, before being 'rescued' from the lake's northern shores by the convict Graham. This local legend inspired sensational nineteenth-century newspaper reports, and later Patrick White's novel *A Fringe of Leaves*. Fraser's belief that the Indigenous people – who fed and treated her with traditional medicine – had kidnapped rather than rescued her, fitted her European contemporaries' prejudices and preconceptions. The incident increased hostility and mistrust on both sides of the Queensland frontier, and paved the way for the violent dispossession that followed.[23]

There is no monument to those who kept Eliza Fraser alive.

When Judith Wright's poetry was first foisted upon me as a schoolboy in the 1990s, she was still being taught as a jingoistic nationalist. The focus was on early poems like 'Bullocky' and 'South of My Days', which could be taken to celebrate the heroic pioneers of Australia's rural mythology. In the classroom, even furiously angry political poems like 'Australia, 1970' were systematically drained of their force by the counting of iambic feet and the labelling of line endings. Wright, ever the prophet, accurately predicted that generations of schoolteachers would turn her poems into 'implements of torture'. That was certainly the case at my suburban state school, where even the handful of us who were keen readers and drawn to poetry decided, on the basis of Judith Wright and a narrow sampling of others, that Australian literature was 'too dusty' for modern city kids. We devoted ourselves to reading Americans and Brits. They seemed to inhabit a larger, more sophisticated universe than our own. It was only in my twenties, when the tough subject matter, formal daring and intellectual energy of Latin American writers set my senses alight, that I began to be curious about writing from my own hemisphere.

Further around the shoreline, past the general store and the camping ground, stands the trunk of a lone paperbark. Knotted white, and dead as many years as I can remember, its branches claw the sky like a witch's gnarled hand. Even when campers' kids play in the shallows around it or kick a ball across sand knobbly with its dead roots, the tree casts an eerie spell over this stretch of beach.

This scorching summer morning we have the place to ourselves. I hold Vera up to see the skeletal paperbark, but recoil when she reaches out for its trunk.

'Don't touch. Not that tree.'

The haunted paperbark has always reminded me of the 'driftwood spear' that startles the narrator of Wright's poem 'At Cooloolah', from *The Two Fires* (1955). It is among her best-known lyrics and became an unofficial rallying cry for conservationists pushing to protect the region from sand mining in the 1960s and 1970s. Returning to it after many years, I realised I'd only skimmed the surface.

The poem is a nature inscription. It commemorates the feelings triggered by a place of natural beauty, beginning with the image of a white-faced heron. Wright refers to it by its common name, the blue crane, capturing the impression that the bird, a greyish-white wader common across

223

Australasia, 'wears' the colour of the evening sky mirrored in the water:

> The blue crane fishing in Cooloola's twilight
> Has fished there longer than our centuries.
> He is the certain heir of lake and evening,
> And he will wear their colour till he dies,[24]

For Wright, the sight of the crane fails to bring 'tranquil restoration',[25] as might be expected in the European romantic tradition. 'Our centuries' stresses the brevity of settler-Australian presence at Cooloola when compared with the crane's timeless belonging. It's not the individual bird whose life has endured centuries, but the species. By repeatedly referring to plural phenomena with singular nouns – 'plumed reed and paperbark', 'crane and swan' – the poem slides from the individual to the archetypical. Birds often symbolise the relationship between the conscious and unconscious mind in Jung's writing – a strong influence on Wright. The poet's unconscious fear, anxiety and sense of unbelonging in the Australian landscape are implicitly registered from the outset and become ever more pronounced. The stanza ending 'till he dies' has an ominous ring in the wake of Wright's epigram from Heraclitus, which describes the world as a fire, 'with measures of it kindling, and measures going out'.[26] This is 1955, ten years on from the bombing of Hiroshima and Nagasaki, with the USA and Soviet Union locked in an arms race. Are the bird, the lake, the poet and her song all about to be extinguished?

The third stanza shifts suddenly from the threatened loveliness of the lakeside scene to violence of another kind:

But I'm a stranger, come of a conquering people.
I cannot share his calm, who watch his lake,
being unloved by all my eyes delight in,
and made uneasy, for an old murder's sake.[27]

What is this old murder? As with the crane, Wright is working from the particular to the general. In talking about one killing, she is referring, in the first instance, to the local fate of 'those dark-skinned people who once named Cooloolah'. It's well known that massacres of Indigenous people took place at nearby Lake Weyba and Teewah Beach during the nineteenth century. But the 'old murder' also stands more broadly for the violent dispossession of Australia's first peoples that was written out of our history over much of the twentieth century. 'At Cooloolah' attends to the mental toll repressing this past takes on the settler-Australian conscience. As the daughter of an old pioneering family, Wright feels personally implicated:

Riding at noon and ninety years ago,
My grandfather was beckoned by a ghost –
a black accoutred warrior armed for fighting,
who sank into bare plain, as now into time past.

The cause of the grandfather's bad conscience becomes clear when we refer to a more detailed version of the same incident in Wright's novelised family history, *The Generations of Men* (1959). Albert Wright, Judith's paternal grandfather, was an important settler in the Dawson Valley district of central Queensland in the 1870s. According to his diaries, he was once called to the scene of a murder of four Aboriginal men. As co-manager of the station and local justice of the peace, it was his duty to inform police. Instead, knowing he would be shunned as a traitor to his fellow white men if he reported the incident, he rode conspicuously back into town, giving the perpetrators time to dispose of the bodies. 'Neither whites nor blacks would ever speak of them again,' wrote Judith. 'But on Albert's mind they stayed a heavy load.'[28] This is the background, in *The Generations of Men*, to the ghostly appearance of 'a warrior standing alone by the one dead tree on the plain'.[29]

In 'At Cooloolah' the grandfather's role as collaborator in a cover-up, rather than a perpetrator, is not spelt out. The reader must disentangle the relationship between old murder, grandfather and ghost for him- or herself. The historian Georgina Arnott argues in *The Unknown Judith Wright* (2017) that, while the poet was among the first to acknowledge the devastation the pastoral invasion of Australia caused to Indigenous people, her writing tends to downplay her own ancestors' role in it. For Arnott, Wright's interpretation of the historical documents suggests 'the enduring strength of a family loyalty that she was not always fully aware or in control of'.[30]

Wright might have been a flawed historian. But her poetry gains much of its charge from the tension between family loyalty, love of the land, and the ethical imperative to acknowledge past wrongs. In 'At Cooloolah', the neat four-line stanzas and regular five-stress lines express a need for containment and control that is undone by the thematic focus on the return of the repressed. Finally, an ancestral curse wells up from the lake water to trouble the conscience of the pioneer-pastoralist's poet granddaughter:

> And walking on clean sand among the prints
> of bird and animal, I am challenged by a driftwood spear
> thrust from the water; and, like my grandfather
> must quiet a heart accused by its own fear.[31]

The spear is the guilt of the historical beneficiary of colonialism, and it is also the fear of the fire that might soon be reflected in the lake's 'clear heavenly levels' in the event of nuclear war. The crane's centuries of fishing may soon be disrupted, it is implied; even this peaceful shoreline will not be spared.

The little we know of Cooloola's earliest inhabitants has been built up by triangulating archaeological evidence, written accounts by nineteenth-century Europeans and testimony from a handful of Aboriginal elders.

Camp entrances faced downwind; grass was scattered on the floors of bark huts; possum-skin rugs were sewn together with kangaroo-tail sinew; they set out inland on daily foraging missions; oysters, fresh fish, scrub turkey, bunya nuts, bandicoots and honey were consumed; children were forbidden to eat eels; the chests and upper arms of initiated men were cut with sharp shells and healed with grease and charcoal; bark canoes were used to navigate waterways; tracks were marked by bending a branch to 90 degrees at hip height; much time was spent gathering firewood; they feared thunder and lightning and would not pronounce the names of the dead; whites were believed to be the ghosts of blacks; the land was believed to have been created by a turtle brooding on the water; the cry of a curlew signalled impending death.

Cooloola, with its infertile soil and dense forests, protected the coastal Dulingbara – the people of the nautilus shell – from Europeans some 25 years longer than their inland neighbours, the Batjala and Gubbi Gubbi, whose traditional lifestyles were disrupted by pastoral settlements along the Mary River and the brutality of the Native Police Force throughout the 1850s. Shell middens and stone artefacts discovered at Cooloola suggest Aboriginal presence for five millennia, with a continuous pattern of occupancy from about 900 years ago until around the time of the 1867 Gympie gold rush. At that time, the demand for building supplies on the booming inland goldfields attracted timbermen to Cooloola's pristine stands of cedar and pine.

The Dulingbara were shipped off to missions or forced from the forest to seek their fortunes in Gympie, where they often died of imported diseases and drink. They were poisoned at Kilcoy and shot near Lake Weyba at a place now called Massacre Creek. In 1950, an elder named Gaiarbau, or Willie Mackenzie, sat down with an anthropologist and recorded his memories of touring the region as a young man in the 1880s – the basis of much of our present knowledge. A few years later, he spoke with Judith Wright's close friend, the Aboriginal poet Oodgeroo Noonuccal, who commemorated their encounter in a poem:

> I asked and you let me hear
> The soft vowelly tongue to be heard now
> No more for ever. For me
> You enact old scenes, old ways, you who have used
> Boomerang and spear...
> All gone, all gone. And I feel

The sudden sting of tears, Willie Mackenzie
In the Salvation Army Home.
Displaced person in your own country,
Lonely in teeming city crowds,
Last of your tribe.[32]

The three of us hike the forest trail out to Mill Point. For the first kilometre or so, Vera gazes into the treetops from the hiking pack on my back, trying to find the whip bird whose song rings out in the canopy. Sunlight slants between the dazzling white trunks of red and scribbly gums, blackbutts and melaleucas. There are plenty of 30- and 40-year-old trees, but nothing older. The forest is still regenerating. By the time we reach the turn-off, Vera's fast asleep. She ignores the mosquitos, and doesn't even wake when a huge grey kangaroo, taller than R, bounds across our path and vanishes into the long grass.

The ruined brick chimney of an old dairy under mango and guava trees announces we've arrived. Along with a few railway sleepers and a rusted-out boiler, this is all that remains of McGhie, Luya and Company's timber settlement. At its height in the 1880s, 60 families lived on the shore of Lake Cootharaba. The township flourished for 20 years, sending Kauri pine and cedar to Brisbane by steamer. But by the 1890s, the best timber supplies were exhausted. Shortly after the mill closed its doors, it was wrecked by the catastrophic floods of 1893. Lake water rose 2 metres over the shoreline.

Judith Wright's 'The Graves at Mill Point' describes the lonely tomb of a timber cutter named Alf Watt, whose passing she imagines as the end of the whole forlorn, windblown little outpost: 'When he died the town died.'[33] The poem unfolds as a dialogue between the poet and the bloodwood tree growing from the dead man's bones: 'Tell me of the world's end, / You heavy bloodwood tree.'[34]

Wright's lyric has sometimes been interpreted as an elegiac tribute to the pioneers who opened up Cooloola. But I'm inclined to read it ironically, as a grim parody of bush balladry. The bloodwoods, with their tear-shaped leaves, only appear to weep for the woodcutters in their graves, and to flower 'for their sake',[35] if we accept the anthropocentric conceit that humans operate outside and above nature. If we believe, as Wright did, that humans are part of nature's web of interdependencies and subject to its laws,[36] then what we have is an image of humanity being cut down to size. The wind in the leaves is less a lament for the timber cutter than a sign of nature's indifference. The trees that outlive the timber town have no cause to mourn its human occupants – they simply go on flowering as they've always done.

Like 'At Cooloolah', the poem uses local history to prophesy apocalyptic consequences for civilisation more broadly, if human beings continue to assert God-like power over nature. The ultimate symbol of this arrogance, for Judith and Jack, was the nuclear bomb. 'The long wave that rides the lake / with rain upon its crest'[37] is an image of a tidal wave sweeping the placid waters of Cootharaba, perhaps even of nuclear rain. The ruined mill is 'where the world ends' in multiple ways. It's situated at the 'end' of civilisation and is where the 'world' of the town ended. But in a final and more drastic sense, the Mill Point timber settlement symbolises the end to which the world will come if humans fail to reconfigure their relationship with nature. As in Wright's more overt poems of atomic anxiety, her fears for the future are embodied in the figure of her daughter, the 'wandering child'[38] who stoops to read Alf Watt's gravestone.

Through roaring wind and lengthening shadows, we hurry back from Mill Point to the sanctuary of the lakeside house.

In 1966, after 15 years 'in the very core of concentration',[39] Jack McKinney finally finished *The Structure of Modern Thought*, his philosophical epic about 'the modern crisis of feeling and of thought'.[40] Though he had written himself out of the personal crisis that had gripped him when he first met Judith, the effort of transforming himself from a soldier-farmer into a published philosopher wrecked his health. He was suffering from rheumatism and severe stomach cramps and had already survived multiple heart attacks. In October, sensing their time together would be limited, the couple took a driving holiday to the 'obscure hamlet' of St George in south-west Queensland, where Jack had worked as a drover in his 'last year of innocence' before the First World War.[41] Half a century on, they found the brigalow country unrecognisable – cleared, ploughed and environmentally devastated. Travelling through this dead landscape, the normally gregarious Jack lapsed into silence.

He was diagnosed with inoperable stomach cancer upon their return and died, two months later, of a heart attack, at Greenslopes Repatriation Hospital in Brisbane.

Judith couldn't bring herself to visit the lakeside house for many years. 'I have not dared to go to Boreen,' she wrote to Barbara Blackman a year after Jack's death.[42] In 1973, she finally returned to sell Melaleuca. Her last Cooloola poem, 'Lake in Spring', attests to the loneliness of this trip, for the shallow reaches of Lake Cootharaba no longer carry Jack's reflection:

> Now when I bend to it again
> another spring, another year
> have changed and greyed the images,
> and the face that lay beside
> my own, no longer answers there.[43]

By the time I returned from my first trip to South America with an unkempt beard, shaggy shoulder-length hair, and a backpack stained with red dust, Old Al was in a high-level aged-care facility near my parents' house. I turned up with a tape deck, intending to record the story of his war service. Though he remembered who I was, he wasn't in any state to coherently recount his life. He kept counting the red vehicles in the carpark and the horses in the paddock behind the back fence.

His dementia was advanced by the time R came into my life. She never met him, but she held my hand through the funeral and that was enough. It was a small service at a Redcliffe funeral parlour with about 30 mourners in attendance. Beyond the immediate family, most were elderly female friends from the retirement village – he had outlived his male friends.

'Your grandfather could have remarried, you know,' said his blind neighbour, leaning on my arm. 'Plenty of ladies were interested.' She shook her head. 'But he was a one-woman man.'

We sat across the aisle from my parents through the speeches. My mum, who'd been at the bedside when he died, calmly outlined his childhood, war service, marriage and long widowhood. My peacenik uncle, up from the commune, wept at the lectern as he tried to convey something of the generational divide that had separated him from his father.

In the absence of any religious rites, the funeral director had asked us to supply a reading. Reluctantly, we settled on 'Clancy of the Overflow' because an old Banjo Paterson anthology was the only poetry we found in his house. From the state of it, I suspected it had belonged to my grandmother and had sat mouldering in the garage for 20 years. Though there was always a stack of popular science by his bed, I'd never seen Al read a work of imaginative literature. As I read the poem aloud for the assembled crowd, its nostalgic depiction of rural Australia seemed remote from the reality of his life. I wish we'd found Judith Wright in his garage instead.

When the ceremony was done, the funeral director asked if I'd like to say goodbye before the body was taken to the crematorium.

'Just be aware,' she said, parting the curtains and leading me towards the coffin, 'that he's been in the fridge. The cold gives some people a fright, but it's perfectly normal.'

He wore a baggy brown suit. His eyes were closed and his mouth was slightly ajar. I lay my warm hand on his cool one and wondered about the things that hadn't made it into his journals. 'Why make a fuss?' was a far cry from

Judith and Jack's overt anti-war activism. But I thought I sensed in his refusal to celebrate Anzac Day an unspoken scepticism, and in his compulsive reading of atheist polemics a quiet unease about the things he'd been made to do as a young man. There were a million German casualties of the Allied bombing campaign in the Second World War, at a cost of 100,000 Allied airmen. Men who refused to fly were classified as 'lacking moral fibre'.[44] Those who did were asked to flatten whole towns. Some of their missions, like the bombing of Dresden, weren't directed at major centres of wartime industry, and instead targeted civilians to break German morale. Having survived the terror of more than 40 night-time bombing missions, and lost many friends, Al had 60 years to reflect on what it all meant.

The director discreetly coughed, eager to clear the room for the next funeral.

That night, I woke up past midnight with the distinct sensation of my grandfather's cold hand gripping mine. One last bone-crunching handshake.

'What is it?' asked R, stirring.

'It's nothing. Just hold my hand.'

Judith's habit of inflating Jack's importance and diminishing her own could already be observed in the early days of their courtship:

> Darling I've just finished typing the article and it came over me all of a sudden on the crest of a great wave of humility that I belong to a very great man...and when my modest name goes down to posterity it will be because I had the honour of typing the first copies.[45]

The year after his death, she persuaded Chatto and Windus in London to posthumously publish *The Structure of Modern Thought*. It was brought out in 1971. Aside from a snobbish dismissal in the *Spectator*, the notices were sympathetic. But none of it added up to the 'intellectual atom bomb'[46] he'd predicted in an early letter. Judith, unlike my grandfather, had a second great love: a 25-year relationship with the high-profile public servant Nugget Coombs. Still, she remained a fierce advocate for Jack's philosophy all her days, and often said her greatest regret was not bringing it to a wider audience. They are buried together in the Mount Tamborine cemetery under a gravestone that reads 'United in Truth'. She insisted all her life that Jack McKinney would have made a seminal contribution to twentieth-century thought, if anyone had cared to listen.

On the evidence of *The Structure of Modern Thought*, it's hard not to conclude that Jack's greatest contribution to twentieth-century intellectual life was the imprint he left in Judith Wright's poetry. However brave, brilliant and charismatic, he was not the neglected giant she believed him to be. He was her muse, I think, in an era when it wasn't acceptable for the woman to be the genius and the man to play the supporting role, even among free thinkers and artists. And he was foremost among the many difficult causes Judith championed over the years.

From the 1970s until her death in the year 2000, Wright's focus shifted from poetry to environmental activism and agitation for Indigenous rights. One of her great early successes as President of the Wildlife Preservation Society of Queensland was the push to protect the Cooloola sand mass from rutile and zircon mining. In 1967, the Bjelke-Petersen state government granted Conzinc Riotinto a permit to mine sections of the 1.8 million year old Cooloola dunes, with operations set to expand within a few years. As the 1972 state elections approached, the WPSQ petitioned the Queensland parliament and targeted marginal seats. Their grassroots campaign, 'Spend Five Cents to Save Cooloola', resulted in 15,000 postcards being delivered to the Premier's office:

> Your government's failure to declare the whole of Cooloola
> a National Park, in the face of mounting public pressure,
> is deplorable. The only acceptable use for this unique
> wilderness is its immediate dedication as a National Park.[47]

Their efforts prompted a backbench revolt against cabinet. Bjelke-Petersen eventually sided with the nervous backbenchers, using his casting vote to save the dunes and his own job. Sand mining ceased in 1976 and the whole of Cooloola is now part of Great Sandy National Park.

Forty years on from that victory, and a couple of years after the centenary of Judith Wright's birth, the ongoing urgency and importance of her work – both as a poet and a conservationist – lies in the way she speaks to global environmental crisis out of the haunted, damaged spaces of the colonised Australian landscape. Gradually – with the translation of her work into Japanese, Russian, Spanish and other languages, and new scholarship like that of Stuart Cooke placing her work in dialogue with Latin American nature poetry[48] – we are coming to recognise Wright as a world poet rather than one who merely explains Australia to itself. She is a poet of our hemisphere – 'this southern weather'[49]– whose themes of environmental destruction and decolonisation resonate far beyond the peaceful beaches of Lake Cootharaba.

So, we lie sleeping in the lakeside house on land that belongs to us but will never be ours. The wind whispers 'Coo-loo-la' in the melaleucas. Vera sleeps on my chest in a room filled with golden light.

Al never set eyes on the lakeside house, but I know he would have loved it: the boatshed and macadamia tree out the back, the breezy eastern outlook from the veranda. Water was always a solace to him. Mum took him to the ocean at every opportunity during the 20 years he lived alone. They had sailed mirror dinghies together on Port Phillip Bay in Melbourne when she was a girl. The lakeside house, furnished with his things, is decorated with seashells and driftwood and Mum's photos of the world's watery places: the Scottish lochs, the Yangtze River, the Aegean Sea. And there, out the window, our shining lake. Beyond its far shore, beyond the thin finger of land separating us from the Pacific, the roar of the ocean breakers is louder; the tide is rising.

It's good to be still, having moved so much these last years. This is Dulingbara and Gubbi Gubbi country, but I'm finally beginning to feel we belong here, too. Outside all is water, light and air. Melbourne, Pátzcuaro, Torreón, Brisbane and Mexico City converge in the voices of the older generation. Sleep's tide takes us. Though we are surrounded by my mother's photos of her travels in the north, our dreams are of the south: the Oaxacan village where the healer made her prophecy; the Patagonian glacier we heard crack like thunder; the cave paintings at Carnarvon of red clay hands reaching out of the past. At the edge of consciousness, I register hands lifting Vera off me, carrying her into the next room.

I wake alone. R's voice floats in from the balcony, speaking to our daughter in soft, childish tones. As I emerge, blinking in the sunlight, I see she has Vera sitting on the broad wooden railing facing the lake. It's a clear morning and the water's surface is 'blue as a doll's eye'.[50] I put my arms around R and give Vera a good-morning peck on the cheek, but she barely acknowledges it, because her eyes are fixed on the undulating sky upon the water where a pelican is about to land. For a moment, it hangs over a perfect mirror image of itself.

Then the two birds merge.

Notes

Requiem with Yellow Butterflies

1 G. García Márquez, *One Hundred Years of Solitude*, G. Rabassa (trans.), Avon Bard, New York, 1971, p. 227.

2 Juan Manuel Santos cited in A. Navarro, '*Colombia despide a García Márquez con Mozart y vallenatos*', *El Espectador*, 22 April 2014, viewed 13 June 2014, <https://www.elespectador.com/noticias/cultura/colombia-despide-gabriel-garcia-marquez-mozart-y-vallen-articulo-488194> (author's translation).

3 Santos cited in '*Gabo vivirá para siempre en las esperanzas de la humanidad: Santos*', *El Espectador*, 21 April 2014, viewed 13 June 2014, <https://www.elespectador.com/noticias/temadeldia/gabo-vivira-siempre-esperanzas-de-humanidad-santos-articulo-488040> (author's translation).

4 J. Cruz, '*Gabo ya no es de este mundo*', *El País*, 21 April 2014, viewed 13 June 2014, <https://cultura.elpais.com/cultura/2014/04/21/actualidad/1398106806_098741.html> (author's translation).

5 Santos cited in Navarro, *El Espectador*.

6 J. Cruz, '*Gabo ya no es de este mundo*'.

7 'Gabriel García Márquez: One Hundred Years of Solitude', *New York Times*, 3 March 1970, p. 39.

8 S. J. Levine, 'The Latin American Novel in English Translation', *The Cambridge Companion to the Latin American Novel*, Efraín Kristal (ed.), Cambridge University Press, 2005, p. 302.

9 Harriet de Onís cited in Levine, 'The Latin American Novel', p. 303.

NOTES

10 G. García Márquez, 'Nobel Lecture: The Solitude of Latin America', Stockholm, 1982, viewed 27 May 2014, <https://www.nobelprize.org/nobel_prizes/literature/laureates/1982/marquez-lecture.html>.

11 García Márquez cited in G. Martin, *Gabriel Garcia Marquez: A Life*, Bloomsbury, London, 2004, p. 565.

12 J. L. Borges, 'The Homeric Versions', *The Total Library: Non-Fiction 1922–1986*, Eliot Weinberger (ed.), Esther Lane et al. (trans.), Penguin, New York, 2000, p. 69.

13 R. Barthes, 'The Death of the Author', *The Norton Anthology of Theory and Criticism*, Vincent B. Leitch et al. (eds), W. W. Norton & Company, New York, 2001, p. 1470.

14 '*La cultura latinoamericana de luto*', *Granma*, 17 April 2014, viewed 13 June 2014, <https://www.granma.cu/cultura/2014-04-17/la-cultura-latinoamericana-de-luto-fallecio-gabriel-garcia-marquez> (author's translation).

15 Mario Vargas Llosa cited in V. Gorodischer, '*Gabriel García Márquez: el mundo despide al gigante de las letras*', *La Nacion*, 19 April 2014, viewed 13 June 2014, <http://www.lanacion.com.ar/1683361-gabriel-garcia-marquez-el-mundo-despide-al-gigante-de-las-letras> (author's translation).

16 H. Fontova, 'Gabriel García Márquez Castro propagandist police snitch', *FrontPage Mag*, 23 April 2014, viewed 13 June 2014, <https://www.frontpagemag.com/2014/humberto-fontova/gabriel-garcia-marquez-castro-propagandist-police-snitch/>.

17 'The magician in his labyrinth', *The Economist*, 26 April 2014, viewed 23 February 2015, <https://www.economist.com/news/obituary/21601223-gabriel-garc-m-rquez-latin-americas-literary-colossus-died-april-17th-aged-87>.

18 P. Carey, 'Like Joyce, García Márquez gave us a light to follow into the unknown', The *Guardian*, 18 April 2014, viewed 13 June 2014, <www.theguardian.com/commentisfree/2014/apr/18/joyce-garcia-marquez-peter-carey>.

Caracas

1 S. Bolívar cited in M. Arana, *Bolívar: American Liberator*, Simon & Schuster, New York, 2013, p. 450.

240

We Want Them Alive

1   E. Poniatowska, '*Regresenlos*', *La Jornada*, 26 October 2014, viewed 1 October 2018, < http://semanal.jornada.com.mx/ ultimas/2014/10/26/201cmexico-se-desangra201d-dice-elena-poniatowska-en-el-zocalo-4330.html/> (author's translation).

2   Felipe de la Cruz cited in P. Ortiz, '*No tengo miedo dice el padre de Ayotzinapa que enfrentó a Peña Nieto*', *Univision*, 8 November 2014, viewed 16 December 2014, < https://www.univision.com/ noticias/noticias-de-mexico/no-tengo-miedo-dice-el-padre-de-ayotzinapa-que-enfrento-a-pena-nieto > (author's translation).

3   Mario César González cited in M. de Lao, '*Padres de los otros 42 normalistas insistirán en la búsqueda, dicen*', *La Jornada Guerrero*, 8 December 2014, viewed 9 December 2014, <https://www.lajornadaguerrero.com.mx/2014/12/08/index. php?section=politica&article=003n1pol> (author's translation).

4   D. Agren, 'Mexico's monthly murder rate reaches 20-year high', *The Guardian*, 22 June 2017, viewed 1 October 2018, < https://www.theguardian.com/world/2017/jun/21/ mexicos-monthly-rate-reaches-20-year-high>.

5   Human Rights Watch, 'Mexico Events of 2017,' *World Report 2018*, 1 January 2018, viewed 1 October 2018, < https://www.hrw.org/ world-report/2018/country-chapters/mexico>.

6   Agren, *The Guardian*.

7   J. Kryt, 'Why the military will never beat Mexico's cartels', *The Daily Beast*, 4 February 2016, viewed 20 June 2016, <https://www. thedailybeast.com/articles/2016/04/02/will-mexico-s-surreal-drug-war-ever-end.html>.

8   E. Poniatowska, *La noche de Tlatelolco*, Ediciones Era, Mexico City, 2002, p. 13 (author's translation).

9   ibid.

10 Poniatowska, '*Regresenlos*'.

11 Investigative Reporting Program, UC Berkeley, '*Iguala: la historia no oficial*', Berkeley, 13 December 2014, viewed 13 March 2015, <https://www.youtube.com/watch?v=yYzy0TRNirEhttps://www. youtube.com/watch?v=yYzy0TRNirE> (author's translation).

12 M. Lowry, *Under the Volcano*, Penguin, New York, 2000, p. 250.

13 ibid., p. 248.

14 D. Hernandez, 'The missing 43: Mexico's disappeared students', *Vice News*, 29 November 2014, viewed 6 January 2015, <https://www.news.vice.com/video/the-missing-43-mexicos-disappeared-students-full-length?utm_source=vicenewsyoutube>.

15 Grupo Interdisciplinario de Expertos Independientes, *Informe Ayotzinapa: investigación y primeras conclusiones de las desapariciones y homicidios de los normalistas de Ayotzinapa*, 6 September 2015, viewed 15 October 2017, <https://www.oas.org/es/cidh/actividades/giei/GIEI-InformeAyotzinapa1.pdf> (author's translation).

16 S. Martínez, '*Los 43 pudieran haber sido incinerados en crematorios del ejercito: especialistas*', *La Jornada*, 4 January 2015, viewed 26 March 2015, <https://www.jornada.unam.mx/2015/01/04/politica/008n1pol> (author's translation).

17 J. Brahms, 'Text: Brahms – *Ein Deutsches Requiem*,' Stanford University, viewed 16 March 2015, <https://web.stanford.edu/group/SymCh/performances/S1995/text.html>.

18 Ezequiel Mora cited in H. Briseño, '*Decreta el gobernador tres días de duelo en memoria del estudiante identificado*', *La Jornada Guerrero*, 8 December 2014, viewed 9 December 2014, <https://www.lajornadaguerrero.com.mx/2014/12/08/index.php?section=politica&article=004n1pol> (author's translation).

19 María Concepción Tlatempa cited in M. de Lao, *La Jornada Guerrero* (author's translation).

Roraima & Manaus
1 B. Chatwin, *What Am I Doing Here?*, Vintage, London, 1998, p. 273.

Don't Care if It Ever Rains Again
1 J. Hernández, *El Gaucho Martín Fierro*, 1872, *La Nación*, Buenos Aires, 2004, p. 6 (author's translation).

2 J. Miller (W. Lane), 'What New Australia is', *New Australia: The Journal of the New Australia Cooperative Settlement Association*, vol. 1, no. 6, 8 April 1893, p. 4.

3 Hernández, *El Gaucho Martín Fierro*, p. 34 (author's translation).

And the Village Was Fair to Look upon
1 M. Gilmore, 'Wild Horses', *More Recollections*, Angus & Robertson, Sydney, 1935, p. 1.

2   'The New Australia Madness', *National Advocate*, 10 June 1893, p. 2, viewed 30 November 2017, <https://nla.gov.au/nla.news-article156672539>.

3   J. Miller (W. Lane), 'Introduction', *New Australia: The Journal of the New Australia Co-operative Settlement Association*, vol. 1, no. 1, 19 November 1892, p. 1.

4   G. Souter, *A Peculiar People: William Lane's Australian Utopians in Paraguay*, 1968, University of Queensland Press, Brisbane, 1991, p. 139.

5   J. Strauss (ed.), 'Introduction', *The Collected Verse of Mary Gilmore*, University of Queensland Press, Brisbane, 2004, p. xxxviii.

6   A. Whitehead, *Paradise Mislaid: In Search of the Australian Tribe of Paraguay*, University of Queensland Press, Brisbane, 1997.

7   Souter, *A Peculiar People*, p. 279.

8   Cosme Cooperative Colony, *Cosme Monthly*, December 1894.

9   Cosme Cooperative Colony, *Cosme Monthly*, February 1897.

10 'Ross's Monthly' cited in G. Souter, 'William Lane (1861–1917)', *Australian Dictionary of Biography*, Melbourne University Press, 1983, viewed 30 November 2017, <https://adb.anu.edu.au/biography/lane-william-7024/text12217>.

11 Cosme Cooperative Colony, *Cosme Monthly*, March 1898.

Redcliffe

1   J. Manifold, 'The Tomb of Lt. John Learmonth, A.I.F', *Australian Poetry since 1788*, G. Lehman and R. Gray (eds), University of NSW Press, Sydney, 2011, p. 385.

Old Peak, Young Peak

1   J. María Arguedas, *Los ríos profundos*, Editorial Horizonte, Lima, 2011, p. 49 (author's translation).

2   R. Darío, *Selected Writings*, Penguin, New York, 2005, p.82 (author's translation).

3   G. de la Vega, *Royal Commentaries of the Incas and General History of Peru: Abridged*, K. Spalding (ed.), H. V. Livermore (trans.), Hackett, Cambridge, 2006, p. 3.

4   T. Cusi Yupanqui, *An Inca Account of the Conquest of Peru*, R. Bauer (trans.), University Press of Colorado, Denver, 2005, p. 2.

5   M. Adams, *Turn Right at Machu Picchu: Rediscovering the Lost City One Step at a Time*, Text Publishing, Melbourne, 2011, p. 172.

6   Arguedas, *Los ríos profundos*, p. 65.

7   ibid., p. 16.

8   H. Bingham, 'In the wonderland of Peru', *National Geographic*, 1913, republished April 2011, viewed 6 October 2015, <https://ngm.nationalgeographic.com/1913/04/machu-picchu/bingham-text>.

9   ibid.

10 ibid.

11 R. Kipling, *Kim*, Penguin, London, 1987, p. 49.

12 P. L. van den Berghe and J. Flores Ochoa, 'Tourism and nativistic ideology in Cuzco, Peru', *Annals of Tourism Research*, vol. 27, no. 1, 2000, p. 13.

13 R. Kipling, 'The Explorer', *Collected Verse of Rudyard Kipling*, Doubleday, Page and Company, New York, 1915, pp. 19–22.

14 Bingham, *National Geographic*.

15 Van den Berghe and Flores Ochoa, *Annals of Tourism Research*, p. 17.

16 P. Neruda, *Confieso que he vivido*, Seix Barral, Barcelona, 1999, p. 195 (author's translation).

17 E. Guevara, *Diarios en motocicleta: notas de viaje*, Ocean Sur, Mexico City, 2004, p. 107 (author's translation).

18 ibid.

19 J. Culler, 'Semiotics of tourism', *The American Journal of Semiotics*, vol. 1, no. 1, 1981, p. 130.

20 Van den Berghe and Flores Ochoa, *Annals of Tourism Research*, p. 17.

21 'Drastic new rules coming very soon for visitors to Machu Picchu', *Peruvian Times*, March 2014, viewed 23 October 2015, <https://www.peruviantimes.com/12/drastic-new-rules-coming-very-soon-for-visitors-to-machu-picchu/21727/>.

22 Adams, *Turn Right at Machu Picchu*, p. 57.

23 J. L. Borges, 'Coleridge's Dream', *The Total Library*, E. Weinberger (ed.), E. Lane et. al (trans.), Penguin, New York, 2000, p. 372.

24 J. A. Flores Ochoa, 'Contemporary significance of Machu Picchu', in R. L. Burger & L. C. Salazar (eds), *Machu Picchu: Unveiling the Mystery of the Incas*, Richard L. Burger (trans.), Yale University Press, New Haven, 2004, p. 120.

25 H. Eakin, 'Inca show pits Yale against Peru,' *New York Times*, 1 February 2006, viewed 19 October 2015, <https://www.nytimes.com/2006/02/01/arts/design/01mach.html?pagewanted=all&_r=0>.

26 R. L. Burger & L. Salazar (eds), *Machu Picchu: Unveiling the Mystery of the Incas*, Yale University Press, New Haven, 2004, p. 1.

27   Alan García cited in S. Calderón Bentin, 'Archaeologies of Empire: colonial Hollywood and the neoliberal academy', in L. D. Nielsen & P. Ibarra (eds), *Neoliberalism and Global Theatres: Performance Permutations*, Palgrave Macmillan, London, 2012, p. 44.

28   *'Cusco: 70,000 visitantes admiraron piezas de Machu Picchu devueltas por Yale'*, *La República*, 4 November 2012, viewed 19 October 2015, <https://larepublica.pe/04-11-2012/cusco-70000-visitantes-admiraron-piezas-de-machu-picchu-devueltas-por-yale> (author's translation).

Uluru: How to Travel Without Seeing

1   A. Wright, 'Is travel writing dead?', *Granta*, no. 138, 2017, p. 93.

2   R. Layton, *Uluru: An Aboriginal History of Ayers Rock*, Aboriginal Studies Press, Canberra, 2001, p. 5.

3   A. Markham, 'Three things you should know about Uluru's Aboriginal name', *Travel Outback Australia*, 2014, viewed 23 October 2015, <https://traveloutbackaustralia.com/uluru-aboriginal-name.html/>.

4   Dick Kimber cited in B. Hill, *The Rock: Travelling to Uluru*, Allen & Unwin, Sydney, 1994, p. 9.

5   B. Hill, *The Rock*, p. 310.

6   M. Cathcart, 'Uluru', in T. Bonyhady & T. Griffiths (eds), *Words for Country: Landscape and Language in Australia*, University of NSW Press, Sydney, 2002, pp. 216–17.

7   A. McClintock, 'Climbing the Rock: why do tourists still climb Uluru?', ABC Radio National, 10 July 2015, viewed 20 October 2015, <https://www.abc.net.au/radionational/programs/offtrack/climbing-the-rock-why-do-tourists-still-climb-uluru/6603640>.

8   T. Griffiths & L. Robin (eds), *Ecology and Empire: Environmental History of Settler Societies*, Keele University Press, Newcastle, 1997, p. 6.

9   W. Gosse, *Report and Diary of Mr W. C. Gosse's Central and Western Exploring Expedition, 1873*, Libraries Board of South Australia, 1973, p. 1.

10   ibid.

11   ibid.

12   ibid., p. 15.

13   ibid., p. 10.

14   ibid., p. 9.

15 Northern Territory Government, *Dual Naming*, 7 August 2014, viewed 19 October 2015, <https://www.placenames.nt.gov.au/ policies/dualnaming>.

16 T. Bonyhady & T. Griffiths (eds), *Words for Country: Landscape and Language in Australia*, University of NSW Press, Sydney, 2002. p. 6.

17 R. Hall, *Journey through Australia*, William Heinemann, Sydney, 1988, p. 6.

18 B. Gammage, *The Biggest Estate on Earth: How Aborigines Made Australia*, Allen & Unwin, Sydney, 2012, pp. 51–3.

19 H. Reynolds, 'Foreword', in B. Gammage, *The Biggest Estate on Earth*, p. xxiii.

20 D. Roberts & Mutitjulu community (directors), *Uluru: An Anangu Story*, Film Australia Limited, 1986.

21 ibid.

22 Mal Brough cited in N. Pearson, 'Remote control: ten years of struggle and success in Indigenous Australia', *The Monthly*, Melbourne, no. 3, 2015, pp. 29–37.

23 D. Malouf, 'Mrs Porter and the Rock', *David Malouf: The Complete Stories*, Vintage, Sydney, 2007, p. 130.

24 National Archives of Australia, *The 1967 Referendum: Fact Sheet 150*, 2015, viewed 26 October 2015, <https://www.naa.gov.au/ collection/fact-sheets/fs150.aspx>.

25 Traditional owners cited in Layton, *Uluru*, p. 107.

26 N. Stephen in *Handback*, The Australian Institute of Aboriginal and Torres Strait Islander Studies, <https://aiatsis.gov.au/ exhibitions/handback>.

27 J. Urry, *The Tourist Gaze*, 2nd ed., 2002, Sage, London, 1990, p. 11.

28 A. Neuman, *Cómo viajar sin ver*, Alfaguara, Madrid, 2010.

Porto Velho & Brasilia

1 A. Monterroso, *Animales y hombres*, Educa, Buenos Aires, 1995, p. 21.

Coetzee in Buenos Aires

1 M. Bail, *Homesickness*, Text Publishing, Melbourne, 2012, p. 243.

2 Instituto Nacional de Estadística y Censos República Argentina, *Incidencia de la pobreza y de la indigencia en 31 aglomerados urbanos*, Buenos Aires, 28 September 2016, viewed 15 November 2016,

<https://www.indec.gob.ar/uploads/informesdeprensa/
eph_pobreza_01_16.pdf>.

3   J. M. Coetzee, *Elizabeth Costello*, Vintage, Sydney, 2004, p. 19.

4   J. M. Coetzee, 'Literatures of the South: Introductory Remarks,'
Literaturas del Sur, speech given at Universidad Nacional de San
Martín, Buenos Aires, 11 April 2016.

5   ibid.

6   J. M. Coetzee, '*Literaturas del Sur: J. M. Coetzee y Nicholas Jose en
UNSAM*', panel at Universidad Nacional de San Martín, Buenos
Aires, 14 April 2015, viewed 25 May 2015, <https://www.youtube.
com/watch?v=qEQuPbclekg>.

7   Coetzee, 'Introductory Remarks'.

8   J. Ley, 'Novelist of the sorrowful countenance', *Sydney Review of
Books*, 7 October 2016, viewed 15 November 2016, <https://
www.sydneyreviewofbooks.com/
the-school-days-of-jesus-jm-coetzee-review/>.

9   J. M. Coetzee, *Foe*, Penguin, London, 2010, p. 158.

Parque Lezama

1   C. Lispector, *Hour of the Star*, B. Moser (trans.), New Directions,
New York, 2014, p. 53.

2   J. L. Borges, 'The Mythical Founding of Buenos Aires', *Selected
Poems*, A. Coleman (ed.), A. Reid (trans.), Penguin, New York,
1999, p. 54.

Such Loneliness in That Gold

1   D. Falconer, *The Service of Clouds*, Picador, New York, 1997, p. 70.

2   J. L. Borges, 'The Moon', *Selected Poems*, W. Barnstone (trans.),
Penguin, New York, p. 379.

3   M. Kodama & M. A. Renard, '*Un Borges para el siglo 21*', panel
at Feria Internacional del Libro de Buenos Aires, 29 April 2016
(author's translation).

4   M. Kodama, interview with the author, Buenos Aires, 8 May 2016
(author's translation).

5   Kodama & Renard, '*Un Borges para el siglo 21*'.

6   Kodama cited in A. Prieto, '*Quien es María Kodama:
la viuda, la elegida, la guardiana*', *Clarin*, 10 July 2006, viewed
28 June 2016, <https://edant.clarin.com/suplementos/
cultura/2006/10/07/u-01285316.htm> (author's translation).

7   Kodama cited in K. Takaki, '*Para mi, Japon era mi padre*',
    La Plata Hochi, 1 February 2013, viewed 25 July 2016,
    <https://www.laplatahochi.com.ar/index.php?option=com_
    content&view=article&id=563:para-mi-japon-era-mi-padre&catid
    =72:entrevistas&Itemid=80> (author's translation).

8   ibid.

9   ibid.

10 Kodama cited in M. Ruiz Guiñazú, '¡Mi padre era más joven que
    Borges!', *Perfil*, 13 January 2013, viewed 21 July 2016, <https://
    www.perfil.com/ediciones/domingo/201317450064.html>
    (author's translation).

11 M. Kodama, interview with the author.

12 M. Kodama, *Homenaje a Borges*, Sudamericana, Buenos Aires, 2016.

13 M. Kodama & M. Pericoli, 'Mr Borges's Garden', *New York
    Times*, 1 January 2011, viewed 28 June 2016, <https://archive.
    nytimes.com/www.nytimes.com/interactive/2011/01/02/
    opinion/20110102_Windows.html?_r=0>.

14 Kodama, interview with author.

15 E. Williamson, *Borges: A Life*, Viking, New York, 2004, p. 417.

16 R. Alifano & A. Vacarro, '*El Borges Que Conocí*', panel at Feria
    Internacional del Libro de Buenos Aires, 22 April 2016 (author's
    translation).

17 A. Bioy Casares, *Borges*, Destino, Barcelona, 2006, pp. 1594–95.

18 J. L. Borges, 'Remorse', *Selected Poems*, W. Barnstone (trans.),
    Penguin, New York, 2000, p. 381.

19 Kodama & Renard, '*Un Borges para el siglo 21*'.

20 J. L. Borges, '*A Leonor Acevedo de Borges*', *Obras Completas*, vol. 1,
    Sudamericana, Buenos Aires, 2011, p. 15.

21 Kodama cited in Ruiz Guiñazú, *Perfil*.

22 Kodama cited in Prieto, *Clarin*.

23 Kodama cited in Williamson, *Borges: A Life*, p. 481.

24 ibid., p. 485.

25 J. L. Borges, '*Los Conjurados*', *Obras Completas*, vol. 3, Sudamericana,
    Buenos Aires, 2011, p. 541 (author's translation).

26 Kodama cited in Prieto, *Clarin*.

27 ibid.

28 J. L. Borges, *Labyrinths*, D. Yates & J. Irby (trans., eds), 1962, New
    Directions, New York, 2007.

29 Kodama cited in G. Mayer, '*Entrevista: Borges, como los antiguos
    griegos, pertenecía a su ciudad: María Kodama*', *Sin Embargo*,

7 May 2016, viewed 28 June 2016, <https://www.sinembargo.
mx/07-05-2016/1656864> (author's translation).

30 ibid.

31 J. L. Borges, '*Epílogo*', *Obras Completas*, vol. 3, Sudamericana,
Buenos Aires, 2011, p. 555 (author's translation).

32 M. Schifino, '*Todo Borges*', *Páginas Críticas: formas de leer y de narrar
de Proust a Mad Men*, Fiordo, Buenos Aires, p.87.

33 N. Gelós, 'Poetic Injustice: María Kodama vs the Lit Scene',
Argentina Independent, 26 August 2015, viewed 28 June 2016,
<https://www.argentinaindependent.com/the-arts/
literature-culture/poetic-injustice-maria-kodama-vs-the-lit-scene/>.

34 Kodama cited in Prieto, *Clarín*.

35 Homer, *The Iliad*, R. Fagles (trans.), Penguin, New York, 1990,
p. 210.

San Miguel del Monte

1 D. F. Sarmiento, *Facundo*, Project Gutenberg, 2010, viewed
12 July 2018, <https://www.gutenberg.org/ebooks/33267>
(author's translation).

The Lakeside House

1 J. Wright, 'The Curtain', *Collected Poems 1942–1985*, Angus &
Robertson, Sydney, 1994, p. 216.

2 J. Wright, 'In Praise of Marriages', *Collected Poems*, p. 152.

3 J. Wright, 'Two Songs for the World's End', *Collected Poems*, p. 107.

4 G. Albrecht et al., 'Solastalgia: the distress caused by
environmental change,' *Australasian Psychiatry*, vol. 15, no. 1, 2007,
p. S95.

5 J. Wright, *Half a Lifetime*, Text Publishing, Melbourne, 1999,
p. 280.

6 P. Clarke & M. McKinney (eds), *With Love and Fury: Selected Letters
of Judith Wright*, National Library of Australia, Canberra, 2006,
p. 83.

7 Wright, *Half a Lifetime*, p. 283.

8 M. McKinney, 'Memoir of Judith and Jack', in P. Clarke & M.
McKinney (eds), *The Equal Heart and Mind: Letters between Judith
Wright and Jack McKinney*, University of Queensland Press, 2004,
p. 9.

9   S. P. MacKenzie, 'Beating the odds: superstition and human
    agency in RAF bomber command, 1942–1945', *War in History*,
    vol. 22, no. 3, 2015, pp. 392–5.
10 Clem Christesen cited in V. Brady, *South of My Days: A Biography
    of Judith Wright*, Angus & Robertson, Sydney, 2006, p. 112.
11 Wright cited in Clarke & McKinney, *The Equal Heart and Mind*,
    p. 26.
12 Jack McKinney cited in Clarke & McKinney, *The Equal Heart and
    Mind*, p. 27.
13 ibid., p. 73.
14 Wright cited in Brady, *South of My Days*, p. 129.
15 J. McKinney cited in Clarke & McKinney, *The Equal Heart and
    Mind*, p. 38.
16 Wright, *Half a Lifetime,* p. 186.
17 Wright cited in S. Walker, *Flame and Shadow: A Study of Judith
    Wright*, University of Queensland Press, Brisbane, 1996, p. 211.
18 J. McKinney cited in Clarke & McKinney, *The Equal Heart and
    Mind,* p. 132.
19 Wright, *Half a Lifetime*, p. 280.
20 E. Brown, *Cooloola Coast*, University of Queensland Press,
    Brisbane, 2000, p. 13.
21 M. Flinders, *A Voyage to Terra Australis*, W. Bulmer and Co.,
    London, 1814, p. 7.
22 J. Wright, 'Phaius Orchid', *Collected Poems*, p. 88.
23 Brown, *Cooloola Coast*, p. 82.
24 J. Wright, 'At Cooloolah', *Collected Poems*, p. 140.
25 W. Wordsworth, *The Pedlar, Tintern Abbey and the Two-Part Prelude*,
    J. Wordsworth (ed.), Cambridge University Press, 1985, p. 34.
26 Heraclitus cited in Wright, *Collected Poems*, p. 118.
27 Wright, 'At Cooloolah', p. 140.
28 J. Wright, *The Generations of Men*, ETT Imprint, Sydney, 1995,
    pp. 58–9.
29 ibid., p. 105.
30 G. Arnott, 'Extract: The Unknown Judith Wright', *Teaching
    History*, vol. 50, no. 4, 2016, p. 21.
31 Wright, 'At Cooloolah', p. 141.
32 Oodgeroo Noonuccal, 'Last of His Tribe', *My People*, Jacaranda,
    Brisbane, 1990, p. 11.
33 J. Wright, 'The Graves at Mill Point', *Collected Poems*, p. 193.
34 ibid., p. 194.

35 ibid.

36 J. Wright, 'Conservation as a Concept', *Quadrant*, vol. 12, no. 1, 1968, p. 32.

37 Wright, 'The Graves at Mill Point', p. 194.

38 ibid.

39 J. Wright, 'The Vision', *Collected Poems*, p. 263.

40 J. McKinney, *The Structure of Modern Thought*, Chatto and Windus, London, 1971, p. xi.

41 Wright cited in F. Capp, *My Blood's Country*, Allen & Unwin, Sydney, 2010, p. 145.

42 Wright cited in Clarke & McKinney, *With Love and Fury*, p. 182.

43 J. Wright, 'Lake in Spring', *Collected Poems*, p. 333.

44 MacKenzie, *War in History*, p. 386.

45 Wright cited in Clarke & McKinney, *The Equal Heart and Mind*, p. 139.

46 J. McKinney cited in Clarke & McKinney, *The Equal Heart and Mind*, p. 146.

47 Wright cited in Brady, *South of My Days*, p. 262.

48 S. Cooke, 'Orpheus in the New World: poetry and landscape in Australia and Chile', *Antipodes*, vol. 24, no. 2, 2010, pp. 143–50.

49 J. Wright, 'For New England', *Collected Poems*, p. 22.

50 Wright cited in Clarke & McKinney, *With Love and Fury*, p. 109.

Acknowledgements

Kind acknowledgement to the Fundación Elena Poniatowska for permission to reprint lines from *La noche de Tlatelolco* (Ediciones Era 2002), Penguin Random House UK for permission to reprint sections from Malcolm Lowry's *Under the Volcano* published by Jonathan Cape (1984) and from Willis Barnstone's translations of two poems by Jorge Luis Borges 'The Moon' and 'Remorse' published in *Selected Poems* (2000), Penguin Random House USA for permission to reprint lines from Robert Fagles translation of *The Iliad* by Homer (1990), Harper Collins Australia and the Judith Wright Estate for permission to reproduce lines from Judith Wright's *Collected Poems*, and John Wiley & Sons Australia for permission to reproduce lines from Oodgeroo Noonuccal's 'Last of His Tribe' (*My People*, 3rd ed. Jacaranda Press 1990).

I am grateful for the support of a University of Queensland Research Scholarship while working on this project.

'Requiem with Yellow Butterflies' first appeared in *Open Letters Monthly* and 'We Want Them Alive' in *1966*. 'Coetzee in Buenos Aires', 'Such Loneliness in that Gold' and 'The Lakeside House' were published in the *Sydney Review of Books*. Much earlier versions of 'Caracas', 'Roraima & Manaus', 'Porto Velho & Brasilia' and 'Parque Lezama' appeared in *Nomadology*.

Thank you to the ACT Writers Centre, the Amenta family, Venero Armanno, Leonard Barton, Rex Butler, Félix Calvino, J. M. Coetzee, Alejandro Cortéz, Mary Cunnane, Arturo Desimone, Helen and Ron Diamond, Roberto Esposto, Delia Falconer, Nigel Featherstone, The Fryer Library, Stuart Glover, Kári Gíslason, Frida Hessel, Ivor Indyk, Gail Jones, Nicholas Jose, Anna Kazumi Stahl, Iris Kennedy, María Kodama, Bronwyn Lea, Meredith McKinney, Catriona Menzies-Pike, Gerald Murnane, the Queensland Writers Centre, Emma Schwarz, the State Library of Queensland, Angela Tuohy, Terri-ann White and the team at UWAP, and Gillian Whitlock.

Love and thanks to my parents, Kim and Barbara; to my *suegros* Juan and Carmen; to the Halford-Itos; and to my darling daughter, Vera. Above all, love and gratitude to Chío, my *chispa*.